Praise for the Author

"Some things never go out of style. Kindness, compassion, listening and caring are as important to the success of a physician today as they were at the birth of medicine. Shareef calls on his years of experience as a consultant to bring the modern insights of teamwork, focus and collaboration to the present day doctor This book is a must read for any medical practice that places a premium on maximizing the patient experience."

— Mitchell Brown MD MEd FRCSC
Plastic and Reconstructive Surgeon, Toronto, ON

"*Beyond Bedside Manner* is a must read for everyone in the field of medicine, from medical students wanting to begin their professional career with a foundation for success, to all the members of an established practice trying to better cope with our changing environment. Shareef's insight and his organization of this book can de-stress harried physicians, who are anxious about how to survive, by giving them the tips to thrive."

— Mary P Lupo, MD
Lupo Center for Aesthetic & General Dermatology, New Orleans, LA

"Shareef Mahdavi is a world expert at knowing the empathetic mindset, awareness, and actions it takes for doctors and their team to build and deliver an experience that will secure the trust of their patients. In his masterfully written book he uses his years of teaching and coaching to chart a clear path for doctors and their team to read, follow, and frequently reference as they grow their patient experience. The key to achieving excellence in medicine is to understand what it takes to deliver a world class patient experience and that is why *Beyond Bedside Manner* is a must for all practices that desire to go to the next level."

— Vance Thompson, MD
Vance Thompson Vision, Sioux Falls, SD

"Mr. Mahdavi is an expert in improving the patient experience and creating new revenue sources outside of health insurance in medical practices. *Beyond Bedside Manner* is a pleasure to read with insights of great value to physicians and anyone interested in great customer service. Interested in better patient care while enhancing revenue? This is the book for you."

— Stephen Wilmarth, MD
Wilmarth Eye, Sacramento, CA

"Great advice is a key success factor in any service business, and ophthalmology is a service business. Shareef Mahdavi is my favorite guru in the never-ending challenge to provide a Ritz Carlton experience for our patients in an era of Motel 6 reimbursement. A daunting task, but one that is absolutely essential to build a successful, sustainable practice today."

— Richard L Lindstrom, MD
Founder, Minnesota Eye Consultants, Minneapolis, MN

"The pearls of wisdom found in *Beyond Bedside Manner* is a culmination of years spent by Shareef building authentic relationships with physicians and always looking for ways to improve the patient experience and outcomes while enhancing the physician's joy of practicing medicine. Shareef clearly shows us that despite the influence of insurance companies, big pharma, hospital systems and others, healthcare is most effective when the doctor and patient are the primary decision makers. The engaged and educated patient can be very impactful in helping to change healthcare from "treating illness" to "chasing health." Shareef's insights and experience will help continue the necessary changes in our healthcare system. This book will be much valued by both physicians and patients and the timing of these words is opportune for a world searching for direction and answers."

— Peter Sneed, MD
Oculoplastic and Reconstructive Specialist, Traverse City, MI

"What an incredible resource for anyone in the medical industry and beyond. The customer experience is something that has been often lost in medicine. The author deftly navigates these muddy waters by providing insight to the reader on creating a culture that places the customer center stage to receive first-rate care. This patient-centric culture will not only provide a better customer experience but also a roadmap for achieving greater success for the practitioner. For anyone wanting to do it better but not sure how to make it happen, this book is a MUST! The author provides a thorough outline of all the things I think matter in changing the culture in each of our practices, all in one quick read. There is a paradigm shift necessary in medicine that is focused on the customer experience and a patient-centric approach...this book provides the path to get there!"

— M Bradley Calobrace, MD
CaloAesthetics Plastic Surgery Center, Louisville, KY

"Shareef Mahdavi knows better than anyone walking the planet about building and creating a truly world-class patient experience that ultimately makes price irrelevant. His insights are simple yet brilliantly effective for any business to replicate and execute. *Beyond Bedside Manner* should be every medical practice's bible."

— John R DiJulius, III
Bestselling author The Relationship Economy: Building Stronger Customer Connections in the Digital Age

"*Beyond Bedside Manner* is a much-needed resource to help doctors bring the world of hospitality into their practices. Treating patients like guests is good for business and good for the soul."

— Chip Conley
Boutique Hotelier (Joie de Vivre Hospitality), Strategic Advisor to AirBnB, and New York Times best-selling author

"Medicine lags far behind every other industry in terms of customer service and honing in on what the consumer (patient) desires. *Beyond Bedside Manner* carefully describes proven methods for any practice, whether small or large, to significantly improve the patient experience, grow their volume, improve their impact in the community, and truly make a difference for their patients. Having put into place many of the recommended practices as outlined, I know firsthand that they work. It has made all the difference for my patients, my staff and the way I practice."

— Aaron Waite, MD
Waite Vision, Salt Lake City, UT

"In a time of unprecedented pressures on doctors from all sides, Shareef Mahdavi's book, *Beyond Bedside Manner*, gives a roadmap for doctors to develop a plan for professional success."

— Timothy Hanley, MD
Cedar Run Eye Center, Traverse City, MI

"Exceptional care is the expectation of every patient. Unfortunately today this does not always translate into an exceptional customer experience in our medical practices. Shareef visited the Alabama Nasal and Sinus Center and literally walked through our front door with us and experienced the flow through our office from first impression to departure. Based on his feedback we have repurposed our "waiting room," focused on the "director of first impressions" and examined every step in a patient's pathway through our practice in order to maximize each patient's customer experience. In his book Shareef unpacks numerous opportunities each of us has to make a more lasting impact in the lives of our patients. Open mindedness and a willingness to change the status quo are critical in not just surviving but thriving in today's competitive medical environment. Thank you Shareef!"

— Michael Sillers, MD
Alabama Nasal and Sinus Center, Birmingham, AL

"*Beyond Bedside Manner* offers a wonderful portfolio of ideas to help you create experiential value beyond measure."

— B. Joseph Pine II & James H. Gilmore
Co-authors of *The Experience Economy: Competing for Customer Time, Attention, and Money*

BEYOND BEDSIDE MANNER

INSIGHTS ON PERFECTING THE PATIENT EXPERIENCE

SHAREEF MAHDAVI

Cover and Layout Design: Story Seven Publishing

First-line Editor: Kennedy Mahdavi
Primary and Proofreading Editor: Alyssa Tschirgi

SM2 Strategic, Inc.
555 Peters Avenue Suite 100 Pleasanton, CA 94566

www.sm2strategic.com

Dedication

This book is for my Dad, who devoted over fifty years of his life as a physician, and for all doctors who want to do better for their patients and their practices.

Table of Contents

Foreword

B. Joseph Pine II & James H. Gilmore

CO-AUTHORS OF
*The Experience Economy: Competing for
Customer Time, Attention, and Money*

Attention. Caring. Circular. Deep. Entertainment. Expertise.
Humane. Influence. Innovation. Knowledge. Longevity. Mem-
bership. Mobile. Passion. People-centered. Purpose. Relationship. Sharing. Social Media. Thank You. Velvet Rope. These are
just a small sampling of the words uncovered when surfing Am-
azon.com for books with "Experience" in their titles. All these
qualifiers, however, describe elements that may exist in any
system of production and consumption. Some may even reflect
mission-critical pursuits for enterprises yielding any economic
offering, be it a commodity, good, or service—the three forms of
output generally recognized by economists.

In our article "Welcome to The Experience Economy" (*Harvard
Business Review*, July-August 1998), and even earlier in a 1997
Wall Street Journal piece entitled "How to Profit from Experience," we presented the argument that experiences represent
a fourth genre of economic output, distinct from commodities,

goods, and services. As we saw it, an Experience Economy —
one in which people increasingly and explicitly pay for time in
places and events—was emerging. Today it's here. The Experience Economy has fully arrived. We admit to feeling a great deal
of gratification when we see others also recognize this reality,
such as when McKinsey & Company released a research study,
"Cashing in on the US Experience Economy," reporting American expenditures on experiences increasing 6.3% annually,
while goods and services are only up 1.6% and 4.7% respectively.

We're delighted to see the many new-to-the-world experiences
that have taken hold in the past twenty years, such as Apple
Stores, Airbnb, TopGolf, and Tough Mudder, to name just a few
examples. We marvel at the thousands of escape rooms, rage
rooms, salt rooms, scream rooms, and countless other genres of
experience now consumed. This shift was no mere fad or trend,
but a fundamental change in the very fabric of advanced econo-
mies: We now consume time most of all.

Shareef Mahdavi embraced this fact in the infancy of the idea.
He participated in our annual *thinkAbout* events, at which we
encountered firsthand Shareef's passion for helping doctors
treat patients and his obvious prowess in bringing his consulting skills to health care. Here was a person who truly wanted
to put more Care into Health Care. We encouraged Shareef
to become a Pine & Gilmore Experience Economy Certified
Expert. In this weeklong intensive training, we saw light bulbs
go off. Shareef was a sponge, internalizing our frameworks and
tools as if his own—exactly what we like to see from those in
our network of Certified Experts!

Then Shareef took the all-important step of translating our
principles and design techniques into methods specifically
developed for application to health and wellness. He partnered
with us to form a multi-client forum (a salon, if you will) of a
dozen refractive eye surgeons, which Shareef led as a means to

verify the efficacy of experience thinking when applied to actual medical practices. The results were truly astounding. So much so that in 2011 Shareef was the recipient of our Experience Management Achievement award, given each year to a person demonstrating exemplary work in enhancing the experiences of a particular industry.

Now, with *Beyond Bedside Manner*, Shareef equips physicians and their staffs with fifty-seven insights, drawn from his years helping medical practices offer better experiences. We echo Shareef's advice to read just one per week, looking to apply lessons learned on an ongoing basis. As you do so, we'd like to offer this perspective: Services are *what you do*, your activity; experiences are *how* you do what you do, to enhance your patients' time, to fill it with memorable moments. Nothing creates a memorable event as readily as providing poor service (people always remember that!); so in pursuing better experiences, you can't walk away from the highest standards of service excellence. But what will distinguish your practice and differentiate your business will undoubtedly be the experiences you create. *Beyond Bedside Manner* offers a wonderful portfolio of ideas to help you create experiential value beyond measure.

Why I Wrote
This Book:

I grew up the son of a pediatrician. My dad was known for his kindness and empathy with his young patients and their all-too-often anxious parents. He practiced in an era where doctors were judged, in part, on their bedside manner, which summarizes the interpersonal skills of the doctor and, by extension, nurses and staff. It became a mainstream phrase used to evaluate doctors on criteria patients understand: listening, empathy, kindness, and tactfulness, among others. It was the de facto customer survey in medicine.

While the need for doctors to exhibit good bedside manner hasn't gone away, the world around them is barely recognizable. The once sacred doctor-patient relationship has had a series of wedges placed in-between the two. Some are obvious. Health insurance has devolved into a bureaucratic nightmare for both parties. Online information has simultaneously made patients more knowledgeable and skeptical of clinical recommendations. And technology, which always promises to improve our lives, often falls short. Anybody using EHR will attest to this, as often will their patients. It's easy to see how the doctor-patient relationship has been severely fractured based on what most of us experience in today's healthcare system as patients, as doctors and as staff members trying to run a practice.

But with every crisis comes opportunity. I wrote this book to help you see your practice in a different light. I've spent the past thirty years working with doctors across multiple specialties. Professionally speaking, I grew up in ophthalmology and have been part of several large trends in medical technology (e.g., LASIK). The rising popularity of self-pay elective procedures across multiple specialties, as well as the rise of concierge medicine in primary care, have fundamentally changed how patients interact with doctors and their staff. And while this book originated from the perspective I've gained as part of the "elective" medical industry, the content applies across the board to doctors regardless of specialty, type of practice or patient demographics.

Every practice today needs to focus on what it can do to increase its value. In the past, that meant adding equipment in order to offer new services or procedures. For both reimbursed healthcare as well as elective services, it still means working to make outcomes safer and better over time. And while it's still important for doctors and their teams to be nice, exhibiting good bedside manner is no longer good enough.

The premise of this book is to give guidance to the entire practice - doctors, administrators, supervisors and front-line staff members - on how to move forward and revitalize the doctor-patient relationship. The promise of this book is that when you commit to improving the patient experience, good things happen.

The lessons I've learned over the years have been distilled into a series of insights. These insights take time-tested principles from the world around us and make them relevant and useful in a medical environment.

Every practice has a patient experience; the problem is that most of them are poor. My goal is to inspire you and your team to improve how you do what you do every day. By virtue of the fact that you are reading this, you already have some ideas as to what you want to do differently in your practice. These ideas likely come from your own personal experiences as a consumer and how you like to be treated. This book will give you additional ideas as well as guidance as to how to make it happen. But the most important reason for writing this book is to help you understand why patient experience is worth the effort to perfect, step by step and day by day.

By focusing on patients beyond their clinical needs and delivering on their customer expectations, you will create an environment that attracts patients who willingly spend their time (and money) at the practice. This will happen naturally, as their patient experience becomes on par with their most memorable customer experiences.

Healthcare has largely been given a pass when it comes to the non-clinical aspects of patient care. Pretty much every other industry has been working feverishly to improve customer service and, increasingly, the overall customer experience. Healthcare environments, especially the medical practice, have lagged far behind. Now is the time to change that. It's already happening, especially in practices with office-based care that patients pay for directly. This is what distinguishes the categories of elective and concierge medicine from traditional reimbursed healthcare.

With the investment of time and a willingness to change, you can absolutely take your practice to the next level in terms of the patient experience. As more and more doctors and their teams do the same, I envision practices reaching out beyond the silos of their own specialty to collaborate with other like-minded practices. I've seen a lot of common ground among refractive eye surgeons, plastic surgeons, dermatologists, concierge primary care physicians and cosmetic dentists. There is a growing body of knowledge to share when it comes to how we "treat" our patients. And the patient experience in your practice is one area of the healthcare system where you do have control.

Doctors who have forged ahead on this path will tell you that the work comprises some of the most challenging and most rewarding aspects of what they do. Like all great accomplishments, transforming your practice requires a dedication of heart and mind more than of wallet or purse. In the end, the practice is healthier, stronger and a more vibrant part of the overall community. I firmly believe that if doctors and staff engage patients in a more meaningful way, healthcare outcomes will improve. This is good for your patients, your practice and for society as a whole.

It's time to move *beyond* bedside manner.

PART I:

Developing the Mindset

Developing the Mindset

Your commitment to go beyond traditional bedside manner becomes a mindset that can have a profound effect on your practice. It will change the way you approach your work each day. This mindset will influence how you interact with patients and how you empower your staff to do the same so the entire practice becomes increasingly patient-driven in all the non-clinical aspects of care.

Having worked with hundreds of doctors across multiple specialties, the benefits they've realized include happier patients, stronger practice culture, and improved economics. The biggest change, however, takes place by expanding your role as a professional physician to include essential business and social concepts that weren't covered in those many years of training. What results from employing the common-sense tactics described in this book is practice growth and a rekindled sense of joy. For some, it's a renewal of why they chose medicine in the first place.

The thought that the patient is a customer may not come naturally to every doctor. When it comes to patient health, medical and consumer issues don't seem to get equal footing. The business of medicine seems to go against the goal of most patient encounters. While doctors - having completed nearly a decade of medical training before going into practice - are highly skilled at diagnosing a problem with a patient, they are often at a loss when it comes to diagnosing areas in the practice that are unhealthy in terms of how they impact patient experience.

Improving the health of the patient experience begins with eliminating archaic, counterproductive trademarks often associated with a medical practice: Telephone answering that begins with "Doctor's office, please hold"; the waiting room; the sliding window. And that's just the beginning of what it means to start moving beyond bedside manner. The focus of the practice gradually expands its dedication beyond quality patient care to also include excellent customer satisfaction.

For most of the past generation, healthcare in the US resembled an environment where the patient was like a non-paying customer, essentially "shopping with someone else's credit card," as described by former Whole Foods CEO John Mackey. Imagine how your buying behavior would change if you knew that somebody else was paying the bill. That's been the tradition in the past among patients and the doctors who provided them services. Earlier in my career, doctors routinely lamented that patients would complain when they told them certain services would have to be paid for out-of-pocket.

In recent years, however, the healthcare environment has changed dramatically, placing an increased responsibility for financing on the shoulders of the patient through higher premiums, deductibles and copayments. The rise in elective self-pay offerings across multiple specialties is evidence of this shift, as is the growth in concierge style practices among primary care physicians where a monthly subscription fee is assessed for access to the doctor. This naturally turns the patient into a customer who is seeking to understand the benefits of what they are receiving in return for their investment. Whether you choose to think of them as patients, customers, clients, guests or another title, make no mistake — that patient is becoming an increasingly savvy consumer when it comes to how they choose their healthcare.

There is now a distinct difference between a doctor's role as healer and the business realities of being a service provider. Both are required for the modern doctor and their medical practice. You can overcome whatever biases or preconceived notions you have about what it means to treat patients and serve customers. Below is an exercise that should prove helpful.

Imagine that you have two different pairs of glasses resting on the table in front of you. Your instinct is always to reach for the sturdy pair of black glasses on your right, which helps you as a doctor to see your patient. Using these glasses you can spot ailments from a mile away, noticing the subtlest of symptoms and finding the most accurate diagnoses. But what would happen if you tried on the glasses to your left? These glasses help turn you into a businessperson by looking through the eyes of a customer. With these lenses, you suddenly notice how cold and unwelcoming the front lobby is, or how some staff members get short with patients when stressed. These glasses could become a priceless tool in your toolbelt if you could get used to looking through them. Seeing from a customer's perspective is the first step towards creating a well-rounded, business-savvy practice that looks attractive no matter what glasses you're looking through.

Adjusting to this new frame of mind takes practice and an active desire to improve. Here are three rules of thumb to keep in mind as you consider making patient experience a priority in your practice:

First, you operate in a society where much power is now in the hands of consumers. As overall quality of goods and services has improved across all industries, competition has required businesses to shift their differentiation from what is delivered to how it is received. In essence, power has shifted to the consumer, enabled in part by the immediacy and visibility afforded by the internet. This also helps explain why more and more attention at companies is being given to customer experience.

Second, you are a customer and know how you expect to be treated. You know how it feels when you receive great service as well as how you feel when you get poor service. And you tend to easily recall your most memorable experiences.

Third, every patient is also a customer and, like you, has their own set of expectations. The line has been blurred between patient and customer, and it is your role to serve the needs of both while recognizing that without customers you do not have a practice where you can treat patients.

The next section contains insights that reinforce these three points, putting you on the path of developing a practice that is as exceptional in its customer care as it is in its patient care. This is what it means to be perfecting the patient experience.

As you embrace the concept of people coming to you as both patients and customers, everything you do in your practice going forward flows from the question, "Is this good for the customer?" Inspiration for your practice can come from outside of healthcare, drawing upon retail, hospitality, dining, and entertainment – all industries that are highly focused on meeting the needs and wants of their customers.

By learning from companies that have long worked to perfect their customer experience, you will be ahead of the game when it comes to your practice. And you will discover what they already know: Memorable customer experience creates the virtuous cycle that will build and sustain the business.

THE CYCLE OF GREAT CUSTOMER EXPERIENCE

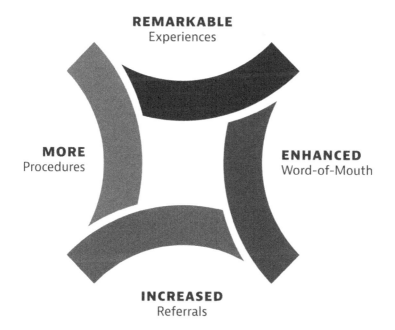

REMARKABLE
Experiences

ENHANCED
Word-of-Mouth

INCREASED
Referrals

MORE
Procedures

How to Read
This Book

Beyond Bedside Manner is designed for everyone working in the medical practice. Staff members should read it as well as doctors. Allow the insights to stimulate discussion among the team. This book can become the catalyst for change in your practice! Recognize that successful practices, like great brands, are built over time, not overnight.

In my experience, serving the customer-driven needs of your patients is the best way to differentiate your practice. As you read these pages, allow insights to sink in. Choose to work on those that resonate the most. Your own motivation to do more will increase as you notice the reaction of patients. Once the patient experience catches fire, it will forever change how you see your practice and its broader mission.

These insights were written to provide at least one new idea each week, categorized into six different areas that affect and influence your success and the value you create for your patients and your practice.

You will determine the pace of change and which insights you believe will deliver the most impact. You can return and find ones that didn't make sense at first but emerge later as opportunities to build on earlier success. There is no specific order in which they need to be approached, so go after the ones that resonate most when you first read them.

Once you've taken the time to read some of the insights and decide which appeal to you the most, you can move on to Part III which introduces a model of change. This simple yet powerful tool will help frame the specific steps you and your staff need to take in order to create change that is built to last.

One last request: as you read through the following pages, give yourself permission. Permission to change, permission to try, and permission to fail. Some of these ideas will be easy to implement; others require more time and effort. Some will seem obvious while others may seem too far a reach. What I've learned over the years is going for little victories and small wins is a good way to start and build confidence in yourself and your team.

PART II:

Discovering the Insights

DISCOVERING THE INSIGHTS

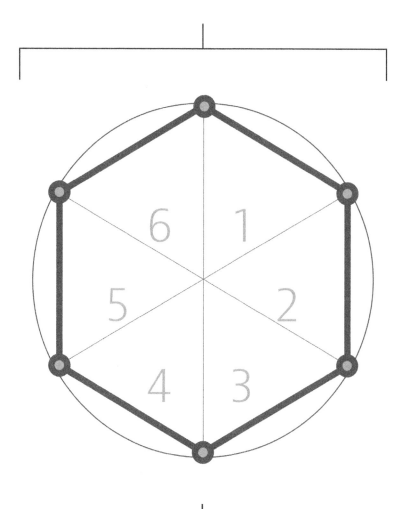

1| PROFESSION 4| PLACE

2| PATIENTS 5| PROMOTION

3| PEOPLE 6| PRICE

PROFESSION

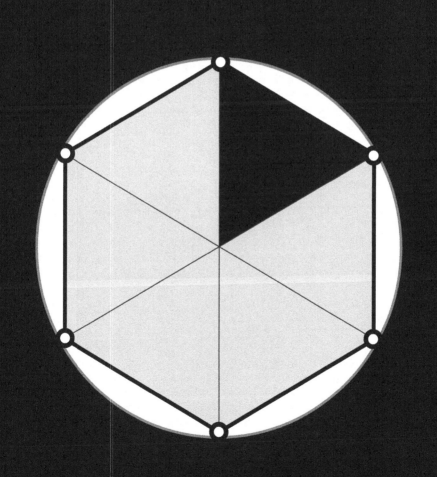

PROFESSION

Your choice to become a doctor is one that wasn't taken lightly and required tremendous sacrifices of time, including most of your twenties. Thinking back, you had a vision of what being in practice would be like. The years have passed and patients are now coming in with customer-like demands, wanting their experience at a medical practice to be on par with other parts of their daily lives. These insights are meant to help you revisit what it means to be a doctor in this new era. The medical landscape has changed significantly since you chose to become a doctor. So has the opportunity to re-write the script so that you not just survive but thrive going forward in your chosen profession.

ONE

What Business Are You In?

From a professional standpoint, this is perhaps the single most critical question you need to answer. Perhaps you never thought of your career this way, given that you went into medicine. But every doctor in practice benefits by thinking about how patients view what they do, and those criteria extend far beyond the clinical interaction. With the rise of the consumer comes an increase in their expectations surrounding all their encounters, including seeing the doctor.

 If you've never consciously considered this question, now is a good time to do so as you contemplate what you want the patient experience in your practice to be. And if you have answered this question, it's worth revisiting as you have an opportunity to upgrade your response. Do you provide a service? Do you also intentionally design a customer experience? Or do you go even further and serve to guide a patient's transformation? How you answer this question impacts most decisions you will make from here on out as to how to run your practice. Ultimately, it defines the value you are able to create as you grow your practice.

Done well, the answer to "What business are you in?" or (more likely) "What do you do for a living?" can serve equally as well at cocktail parties and as a mission statement for you and your team. Indeed, it should aim to be aspirational rather than simply functional.

 " EVERY DOCTOR IN PRACTICE BENEFITS BY THINKING ABOUT HOW PATIENTS VIEW WHAT THEY DO, AND THOSE CRITERIA EXTEND FAR BEYOND THE CLINICAL INTERACTION."

One of the best examples is from an audiologist who answered this question, "I'm in the communications business." He is one of the top customers of a major hearing aid manufacturer and practices in a rural community in Oregon. While he could have simply described the goods ("I sell hearing aids"), the service he provides ("I test hearing") or the benefit provided from a great customer experience ("I help people hear better"), this audiologist understands that at a higher level, he is helping people communicate better. For those with hearing loss, the ability to interact with the world more fully through improved communication is the ultimate value proposition. The audiologist serves as the guide in a transformational experience.

This description of the business is far more powerful and has resulted in a bigger, better and more profitable practice.

So, what business are you really in?

Elevate the description of your business to better reflect the ultimate value you bring to the lives of your patients. This requires thinking beyond the functional services you provide – similar to what others of your specialty do – and heading towards the benefits, as well as the value your patients receive.

Fellow CEEE (Certified Expert on the Experience Economy) Kevin Dulle takes this concept a step further by stating that the business you are in is defined by the primary question you ask your customer. Because healthcare is a services business, the basic question would be "What can we do for you?" As you strive for greater value, an experience-focused practice would ask the patient, "What do you want to do?" An even higher level of value can be attained if you recognize that you are in the transformation business, where the key question your practice would ask is "What do you want to become?"

TWO

Developing
CONFIDENCE

If you could boil down to a single word what patients want to feel after meeting with their doctor, that word is CONFIDENCE. Patients come to you because of your expertise, seeking your advice and medical recommendation. They have heard or read about a specific procedure and arrive with an incomplete set of information. They seek your input as it pertains to their specific goals, needs and clinical qualification.

All too often, the physician's competence is not matched by confidence — meaning the confidence the patient places in you. Their confidence in you is influenced in two main ways.

First is your interaction with them. Being a good communicator means far more than being a good talker. Patient perception is being formed from everything you say (words) to how you say it (tone and emotion) to the clothes you wear and the location of this discussion (e.g., exam room, your private office). Perhaps the largest non-verbal communicator is eye contact; patients notice when you make it and notice it all the more when you avoid it. The precious few minutes they have with you are critical. Their time with the doctor is when they pay very close attention, wanting to resolve the tug of war that is going on in their brain as hope and fear battle one another in terms of decision-making regarding your recommendations.

Second is interaction with your staff and the office environment. Perceptions are being formed upon arrival. And in many practices perception gets lost in translation between your intent and what they see. Your goal may be to offer Nordstrom-like service. But if the office more closely resembles Walmart, patients will perceive your practice like Walmart. Everything surrounding the doctor-patient interaction must be coordinated and harmonized in order to gain their trust and confidence in you. Their perception, not yours, is reality.

Your entire practice is being evaluated by each patient from the moment they enter your practice — be it in person, on the phone, or on your website. You would be wise to invest time improving presentation skills, negotiation skills and even basic communication skills. Each of these feed into building confidence in you and your team that can be seen, felt and heard by patients. All verbal and non-verbal cues should work together to help your patient believe that the skill and caring provided by you and your team will help them reach their goals and make them glad they chose your practice.

THREE

Being
AUTHENTIC

Authenticity has emerged as a principal element people want from their experiences as customers. Just read any article on the purchase behavior of millennials; you will find the word "authentic" used more than once. This sentiment is not limited to the millennial generation. It is permeating what we are looking for in a world where the experience provided is more distinguishing than the service itself. Increasingly, consumers say they are seeking authentic experiences. Social scientist Virginia Postrel summed it up in describing that consumers are shifting their purchase decisions from an object-focused "I like that" to a more personal value-focused "I'm like that." In other words, they want their buying to reflect who they are, right down to core values.

For you and your practice, there are big picture implications as well as specific touchpoints to address. The big picture of your practice should reflect a set of core values that are important to you...and hopefully to your patients as well. One of the big mistakes made by doctors is trying to appeal to everybody. You want patients to be satisfied with their care and loyal to your practice. But as successful marketers know, the key to this is to narrow the focus and attract those patients who are most aligned with your style of practice. This affinity naturally translates to greater appreciation for what you do and an increased propensity to talk to others about their experience as a patient. One example is a local personal training studio in my town called Body Balance. Their coaches' encouraging can-do atmosphere attracts a wide-range of ages and abilities, yet they've developed a successful niche by focusing on meeting the fitness needs of people seventy years of age and above. By focusing more narrowly they've been able to greatly expand their business.

One of the specific touchpoints that should be revisited is the thank you gift that is often given to patients, especially after a self-pay elective procedure. On the surface, you want to show your appreciation for their patronage. Many patients will tell you or your staff they appreciate the coffee mug, t-shirt or other logo-emblazoned item you provided. But through the lens of authenticity, this type of gift can come across as a self-serving means of promotion and ends up in the trash or donation pile. It becomes a line item in your marketing budget with questionable effectiveness.

What if the practice-branded item was replaced with a charitable donation on their behalf to a cause that is important to you? This change can represent a more memorable way of saying thank you. By adjusting the focus of your marketing, it also shifts patient perception with a more authentic way of communicating and reinforcing who you are and what you value.

FOUR

Establishing
CONNECTION

You are likely familiar with Zappos, an online store that started with shoes and grew rapidly over a ten-year period before being acquired by Amazon in 2009. Zappos billed itself as a "customer-service company that happens to sell shoes." Over the years they've built a high level of trust with consumers, making it easy to both purchase and return (they were the originators of "free shipping" that is now standard for online commerce).

What is more remarkable about Zappos is how they train their employees, especially those that are on the telephone all day. As a member of the Customer Loyalty Team (note how different that sounds versus the Customer Service Department), employees are told that the singular goal of each phone call is to establish a PEC, which stands for Personal Emotional Connection. By design, team members are not given a script, a time limit or a quota for how many calls they need to process. They are focused on helping the caller regardless of the nature of the inquiry. This is the approach you should take with your patient relationships. The emotional connection, driven by the feelings that get stored in long-term memory, is a critical part of the doctor-patient relationship. Because patients clearly remember how you made them feel, how you treat people as customers is just as important as how you treat them clinically as patients. Some might argue that the customer treatment is even more important, given that clinical expertise is assumed by the lay person, who is better-suited to evaluate you on everything non-clinical, comparing against other experiences and environments.

Always remember that human behavior – including your own – is driven by emotion and then supported by logic. When considering your clinical recommendation, patients are in an emotionally charged state (hope and fear) and are looking for reasons (i.e., logic) to support the underlying emotion in deciding to move forward or not with the treatment plan.

In the past, doctors were judged in part by their bedside manner, loosely defined as being nice to the patient. For the doctor, being nice is not enough. You and your team want to establish a personal connection with each patient and be on the lookout for anything that can interfere with that emotional interface.

FIVE

Defining
EXCELLENCE

Most doctors define quality in terms of clinical outcomes and what they are able to deliver to their patients. From your perspective, this is what is most important and how you would describe excellence in your practice. Your patients, however, define quality in broader terms. They want and expect a great outcome. They also want and expect to be treated a certain way by staff and feel welcomed in your environment. The criteria they use are the same ones you use whenever you walk into a store, restaurant or hotel. Is it clean? Are the staff nice? Does this match what I've heard about the practice or seen on their website?

While these may seem like basic requirements, they are often lacking in medical environments because the doctor has focused solely on the outcome and not on the "other stuff" that didn't seem to have any impact on the clinical outcome. The "other stuff" is often the determining factor for whether a patient becomes a raving fan, just another satisfied patient or chooses not to return to the practice.

Your outcomes are expected in the same manner that your expertise is assumed (like that of the airplane pilot). While this can be difficult to reckon with for surgeons who have dedicated their career to excellent outcomes, technological innovation in medicine has begun to level the playing field when it comes to outcomes. Software-driven diagnostics as well as surgical tools are designed to reduce surgical variability, meaning there's usually another doctor out there in your community who can promise similar results to yours.

If you've been able to distinguish your practice based on surgical results, that's great. But as excellent outcomes are expected to begin with, this competitive advantage will only dissipate with time. Unfortunately, outcomes are gradually becoming a hygiene factor, a marketing term describing an element that is noticed only if it's missing or something goes wrong.

If you want an army of fans out there referring new patients, seek to determine what can be true motivating factors that cause people to talk about you...in addition to the great outcome they achieved. Motivating factors can be found in the non-clinical customer service aspects of your practice and can become part of redefining what makes your practice unique and special. Just beware that today's motivator can eventually become tomorrow's hygiene factor (remember the Heavenly Bed at Westin Hotels? Once it was a true differentiating feature; now most hotels have great beds).

When it comes to excellence and quality, there are two views—yours and that of your patients. Their view is the one that matters more, as they are voting with their trust as well as their pocketbook.

DEFINING QUALITY

OUTCOMES

Doctor makes eye contact?

Clean office?

Trustworthy?

OUTCOMES

Appreciative?

Well organized?

Treated kindly?

Beyond Bedside Manner

SIX

YOU Are the Brand

A generation ago, a doctor's main goal in building the practice was to establish a solid reputation in the community among patients as well as other doctors. Marketing one's practice, especially via advertising, was frowned upon and even illegal in many states. Suffice it to say that a doctor's reputation served as their brand. That remains the same today, as reputation is still critical.

There's a lot of confusion when it comes to branding, especially in the marketing efforts of a medical practice. There are many factors that influence the brand of your practice and it's too easy to look back and say "If only we had _____," finishing the statement believing that a specific action would have brought more patients in the door. "If only we spent more money on advertising." "If only we moved to a new location." "If only we bought that new piece of equipment."

None of the previous items are bad decisions by themselves;

it's just that they are not the brand. Here are two memorable quotes on branding that have little to do with marketing and everything to do with what takes place inside the practice: "A brand is the promise of a future experience," noted *The Experience Economy* co-author Joe Pine. Business consultant Tom Peters has preached in his writings over the years that "YOU are the brand."

What these quotes convey is that what you do and how you do it are activities that are far more powerful at brand building than any advertising campaign or slogan. In the context of a medical practice, I would offer that the doctor is the brand. No corporate entity whose name is on the door can replace the role that the doctor and their team play in terms of fulfilling the promise to patients as described by Joe Pine. Even if you are an employed physician working for a large hospital, institution or private-equity backed enterprise, there is simply no substitute for the interaction between a doctor and patient.

Building your brand is hard work. It involves making sure your team understands and believes that patient experience can be enhanced in a way that makes the practice extraordinary in the minds of your patients. Building your brand also requires you to make sure you are taking care of the biggest assets in your practice, which are its people. Keeping yourself in shape physically as well as emotionally, mentally, spiritually and financially are personal best practices to keeping your brand healthy. Tending to the needs of what my colleague Vance Thompson, MD describes as his "work family" is equally important to maintaining your brand.

Building and maintaining your brand often means putting a priority on "investing in self," no different than what this book recommends in how you position elective services to prospective patients. Whether it's a personal trainer, an

43

executive coach, or a motivational class, these investments in your *self* will pay future dividends to the brand equity for your practice. Everything else you do to grow the value of your brand flows from these two core activities of building and maintaining.

PATIENTS

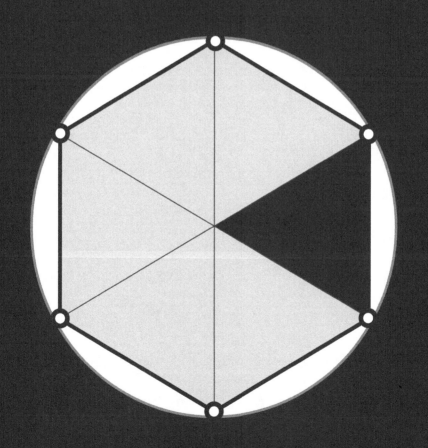

PATIENTS

Your chosen profession indicates that you want to serve the medical and health related needs of patients. As a doctor, you learn to understand your patient medically, diagnosing their ailments then recommending and performing treatment. Your patient also has needs as a customer that go beyond your clinical expertise. They want to be treated a certain way, respected as a human being as much as they are as a patient. Today's healthcare system makes this too easy to forget. What follows are a series of insights to help you better understand your customers and what they really want.

SEVEN

What Patients Really Want

As consumers, patients have an ever-expanding range of choices in how they spend their time and money. You may have been taught that patients come to see you because they have a problem and want you to fix it. Most likely they could have chosen to see another doctor in your specialty. They chose you.

It is now time for you to go beyond this functional reason for interacting and understand what patients value on a deeper level. As in any type of relationship, patients are ultimately people who want to be heard and appreciated. It's that simple. And because so much of what used to take place person-to-person has given way to automation (think ATM versus the bank teller or self-serve gas versus the pump attendant), patients crave a relationship with their doctor. In a world where we no longer have to interact with people for many services, the doctor-patient relationship remains a steady thread of human connection.

"YOU NEED TO LEARN ABOUT WHAT THEY WANT BEFORE YOU START OFFERING WHAT YOU HAVE."

Use the trend towards automation of services as an opportunity to distinguish this relationship as sacred. Think about how your practice can become more human by doing more listening. The more listening you do, the less talking you will need to do. Ignore the rhetoric about how much time this requires. The data are clear that patient satisfaction isn't tied to how much time you spend; it is directly related to how you interact with patients during that time. It's amazing what happens when you are able to uncover a patient's goals and desires. You will vastly improve the foundation of trust between you and your patient. If they trust you, they will listen to you. And the best way to build trust is to "listen first, speak last," a short take on author Stephen Covey's "seek first to understand" habit from his seminal work *The Seven Habits of Highly Effective People*.

When it comes to how you educate patients about your services, begin by asking questions that focus on the patient and their goals. You need to learn about what they want before you start offering what you have.

The best advantage a human has over technology is empathy. Only a fellow human can truly understand the hardships of the human experience. Embrace that particular qualification and figure out how you can validate your patients at an emotional, empathetic level. The more you support your patient through listening and clarifying that you understand what they're saying, the stronger your doctor-patient relationships will be. A patient doesn't come to the doctor solely for medicine, but for the face-to-face assurance from a trusted professional that they will see better, look better, smile better, or feel better. Whatever the specific procedure, our role in this relationship is to help the patient live better.

EIGHT

Achieving Differentiation

If you are in private practice, then you are running a business that also happens to be a medical practice. Pretty much every business you encounter aims to be profitable by serving the needs of customers. If it were only as easy as that sounds when you say it! You've heard stories about doctors who open up an office and build a practice simply by being in place. That was enough to be successful in the era when insurance paid most of the bill, patients had wide access to providers, and the health-care system wasn't nearly as chaotic as it is today. Unless you are in a geography that is highly underserved, that strategy of "build it and they will come" is likely to fail, as competition – for patients, contracts and even reputation — can be fierce even in smaller market communities.

Competition is a good thing, even in the business of medicine. It forces you to continuously seek ways to improve not only in clinical skill but in how you run the practice. Doctors and practices that are leaders in their marketplace have achieved what marketing professionals call *differentiation* in the mind of their target audience. What you might have thought of as reputation for outstanding clinical care has expanded to encompass a larger set of variables, all of which are impacted by your customer service and the overall patient experience.

Like most businesses, doctors need to consider how they want to differentiate what they offer from similar practices. It is not realistic to be all things to all people; you need to determine what you stand for and how you want to be perceived by your patients, other doctors and the community. Marketers call this a positioning statement, and it can serve to guide you in determining what resources and programs are worthwhile investments to grow the practice.

Sadly, too many doctors go straight from drafting a positioning statement to an advertising campaign. The logic goes something like this:

"I am the best at what I do and want patients to choose me because of my superior training. I will advertise my services and focus on my background. They will read this, understand it, believe it, and call the office to schedule an appointment."

Just look at some ads run by doctors and you will see this as a recurring theme. The problem is that today's consumer isn't buying that message. "Trust me, I'm a doctor" as an opening line is no longer credible. Access to information online makes it easy to see what other patients are saying about you as well as to find that same information on other providers in your specialty. Thus, just saying you're good doesn't make it true in the eyes of the patient.

Therein lies a key dilemma facing every doctor: What can be done so that patients choose our practice over others? The goal here is to understand the importance of achieving differentiation in the minds of potential customers so that enough of them choose to be your patients.

While your training is important, it's not a strong differentiator. This is mainly because your expertise is assumed, much in the same way a pilot's expertise is assumed every time you walk onto an airplane. In the patient's mind, training and background are important but viewed as part of what they are getting when they go to a doctor.

Practices that invest in new technology find that it provides differentiation, but only temporarily. They invest time and money promoting a new procedure or device and often find that it pays in terms of attracting new patients as "The first practice in the area to have..." or "The only doctor in the area trained to perform..." But from the perspective of the company that sold the technology, is the goal to have only one practice using their product? No way! They are going to leverage those first successful sales in the area and its success for the practice to convince other competing practices that they too need to offer the same procedure or technology. Over time, if the technology ends up gaining acceptance, more and more providers will have it. If it becomes the standard of care, every practice will eventually offer it. When enough doctors and practices use it routinely, that differentiation is gone.

Some practices believe that using price can be an effective means of attracting customers. A below-market fee schedule or (more commonly) the use of discounting can work to differentiate your services, but at what cost? Do you want to be known as the cheaper doctor in your community? Some might view this as admirable, even noble, in this era of opaque pricing for healthcare services. But if you want to establish your practice as a high quality enterprise, the negatives of low price from a reputational standpoint far outweigh the positives. That time and effort could be spent much more productively by aiming for the highest form of differentiation: patient experience.

Building a practice that is known by patients for an outstanding customer experience will differentiate you beyond your imagination. In part this is because the standard for customer service in medical practices is so low! Doctors have been able to get away with poorly designed "waiting rooms" (who wants to wait for anything anymore?), receptionists that can hide behind sliding windows, and staff that may be competent but lack basic social skills. Investing time and energy into redesigning your practice in terms of its attractiveness to customers will cause you to re-think a lot of how you do what you do and force you to question why you've always done things a certain way. The mindset described in Part I, is a new lens through which to view your practice, but it's a familiar lens that you use everyday as a consumer. You are now simply encouraged to apply this lens to your professional life much as you already do in your personal activities.

While an initial foray into this area will yield a treasure trove of opportunity, this is not a "quick fix" approach to practice improvement. Doctors who are on the path will tell you that in many ways this is more challenging than clinical and surgical work. The rewards are magnified in terms of how patients and staff respond as a growing sense of customer centricity starts to take root and electrify the work environment. Again, this is sufficiently rare in medical environments, so that when you do something to improve the experience, it gets noticed! This is the type of differentiation you want to strive for, where the patients find the basics of customer service (timeliness, cleanliness, communication) are covered and the overall experience is perceived as unique and memorable and...*different* than what they have come to expect when going to see the doctor.

57

DIFFERENT WAYS TO
DIFFERENTIATE YOUR SERVICES

Clinical Training and Skill	Assumed and difficult for patient to assess
Technology	If successful, will be adopted by others
Price	Death Spiral – "Race to the Bottom"
Patient Experience	Defensible and Sustainable – requires commitment

NINE

Read the Reviews...Because Your Patients Do!

Before online reviews became mainstream, a number of doctors I spoke with bristled at the notion of patient comments being posted on a public forum. It was acceptable to send a thank you card or a complaint letter, communications which could be confined to a display area in the practice or to a file cabinet for safekeeping. But the idea of leaving yourself open to public forums of critique was not inherently appealing. Although practices will often still showcase notes and cards of appreciation, the days of keeping such information contained are behind us.

Online reviews, made a societal norm by sites such as Amazon and Yelp, have become highly influential over the way that consumers shop. Reviews of restaurants, which used to be the exclusive domain of food critics, have given way to the crowdsourced opinions of everyday dining patrons. These aggregated opinions of the masses tend to carry more weight than that of a lone expert. A poll conducted by Binary Fountain finds that 95% of respondents find online reviews somewhat or very reliable; 70% say that online reviews influenced their choice of physician.

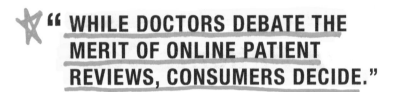

" WHILE DOCTORS DEBATE THE MERIT OF ONLINE PATIENT REVIEWS, CONSUMERS DECIDE."

One doctor in North Carolina attempted to halt this trend by having his patients sign a document waiving their right to post information online. First Amendment aside, that's just a bad idea. It misses the point of reviews in the first place, which is to provide feedback – positive and negative – that should help the vendor, merchant or (gasp!) doctor improve the level of service provided.

While doctors debate the merit of online patient reviews, consumers decide. To be fair, there is a salient difference in healthcare. Unlike restaurants or movies, consumers seeking medical care typically engage with a much smaller sample size of doctors. Let's face it, a young mother isn't going to visit ten to twenty different pediatricians in order to find someone to examine her child. Furthermore, patients are typically not good at assessing the clinical skills of a provider (except perhaps in cases of gross negligence or judgment). However, patients are extremely adept at describing what takes place in the customer service aspects of a medical appointment and indeed relate them to other experiences they have as consumers.

61

The rise of the internet and its ability to facilitate online reviews is part of a larger rise in consumer empowerment. Where in the past information was more tightly controlled by the supplier, be it an automobile manufacturer, hotel chain, or medical practice, it is now readily available in all forms - pricing, availability, quality, etc. This shift has taken place across virtually every industry; healthcare was just a bit late to the party and got a temporary pass while other industries were forced to improve quality of the service as well as cost of the goods produced. Rather than resist, doctors should embrace this trend and use it to their advantage.

Great websites built by firms such as DoctorLogic go much farther in facilitating how practices post reviews, avoiding the temptation for cherry-picking by posting only positive reviews (which is not recommended as it violates the notion of authen- ticity); their platform continually monitors the internet for every new review, bringing them to the attention of the prac- tice in real-time.

While practices should strive for every patient encounter to be an experience that generates a 5-star rating, reality dictates otherwise. Some patients won't be happy no matter what, but their critiques may still offer commentary that can lead to real improvements for future patient encounters.

That data is worth consuming if your goal is to continuously improve the customer experience for your patients. You want both the good news and the bad news. Patients reading the reviews are savvy enough to sift through patient comments and discount those that seem arbitrary or downright mean. Surveys have shown that having a perfect rating leads to suspicion rather than validation; some percentage of lower-than-perfect reviews is deemed as more credible.

We also know that just about every healthcare appointment begins with online research, first to understand a condition and then to find a provider who can help address the need. This is why it's hard to fathom why some doctors either fail to have their own website (and are somehow okay with being listed on a generic Healthgrades page or as part of a hospital directory) or seem to care less about what patients say. That's not smart, as when a consumer scrolling online sees a doctor with only a handful of reviews and an average rating of 1.8 stars, they will simply keep searching to find a medical provider with better reviews.

PERCENTAGE OF CONSUMERS USING ONLINE REVIEWS TO RESEARCH DOCTORS

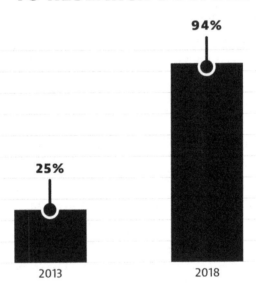

Good reviews are nice; bad reviews can be even better. They represent the voice of the customer and become the data and impetus for change.

Don't allow your ego or bias towards the importance of your work blind you to the reality that you are likely not the only one who can do what you do. Strive for the same excellence in your customer reviews as in your clinical care.

TEN

Mind the Gap

A few years back, the CEOs of three hundred companies were surveyed to learn their perspective on company operations. One of the questions asked for a rating of the customer service provided by their company. 80% of these CEOs rated their customer ser-vice as "excellent." The same question was asked of the actual customers of these companies: only 8% of customers gave a similar "excellent" rating.

Could all these CEOs be "out to lunch" when it comes to custom-er service? Probably not, but this gap is significant and brings up the real issue, which also holds true for most medical practices; our human nature tends to inflate our own self-image relative to how others perceive us. Notable exceptions include family members and pets, who tend to love us unconditionally.

Let's face it. You worked extremely hard to become a doctor and work just as hard to run a practice. Not unlike a CEO, you may have developed an inflated sense of how well your practice is doing from the perspective of the customer. Don't let yourself fall into this trap, as it can prevent you from striving to improve the customer experience. You may be okay if you do nothing in this regard, at least until the average level of service in medical practices improves and forces you to take action. But you likely didn't go into medicine to be average or below average, and recognizing that patients evaluate your customer service as strongly as they do your clinical judgment should be sufficient motivation to commit to working on the customer side as much as you do on the clinical side.

 You are the CEO of your practice. Act like one. And always remember, mind the gap!

DIFFERING OPINIONS ON THE LEVEL OF CUSTOMER SERVICE PROVIDED

	CEOs of the 300 Companies	Customers of the Same 300 Companies
Rated as "excellent"	80%	8%
Rated less than excellent	20%	92%

ELEVEN

Let the Experience Begin

When does the patient experience begin? Most practices would answer that the starting line is when they come in for an office visit or consultation. While that may be the first time they see you, it is not the first experience they have with you. The patient experience began when they first learned about you. Regardless of how they heard about you, they likely went online to search for your name or the name of your practice. After confirming that your patient reviews were acceptable, they went to your website to learn more about you and your practice. Following that, they may have requested an appointment either online or via telephone. Each of these steps constitutes part of their experience.

When does the patient experience end? It doesn't stop when they leave your office; it continues after their visit or surgery date.

In short, there's more to the patient experience than the appointment time in your office.

Innovation pioneers The Doblin Group (Chicago, IL) codified this in their 5E Model on Compelling Experiences. Their framework helps you understand that the customer experience has five distinct stages: Enticing, Entering, Engaging, Exiting, Extending.

FIVE STAGES OF CUSTOMER EXPERIENCE

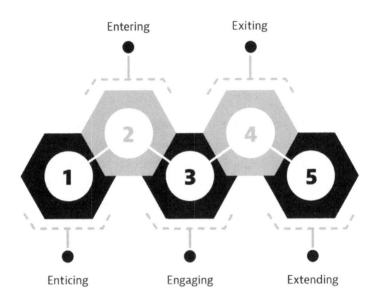

While you may have thought of the in-person encounter as the experience, it's actually the midpoint. Everything you do (or don't do) to entice patients to your practice is part of the initial stage of their experience. They enter your practice when they pull up to your building (or pull up your website), which serves as the warm-up to the main event where they actually engage with you and your staff. This helps explain why plenty of attention should be paid to your website, your parking lot and your front entryway.

At the end of their appointment, do they just exit, or do you have another customer-friendly process to help make the visit more memorable? Doing so is the stage termed "exiting." Finally, those activities you perform to stay "customer connected" serve to extend the experience well beyond the in-person encounter.

Taken as a whole, you can now see that there's far more to the experience than what happens in-person. You have many opportunities beyond the doctor's office to make a strong first impression and reinforce that with a lasting final impression. The best final impression is never really final, because it's all about showing the patient that you are invested in their future with the practice. The more effort you put in what happens when patients walk out the door, the more likely they are to walk through the door again.

If five stages are too many, then think about the experience in three parts: beginning, middle, and end. What's important here is to recognize that impressions are being formed both before and after a patient is actually in your presence.

TWELVE

Keep It Fresh

A patient's decision allowing you to perform a procedure is an act of trust. When the procedure is elective and paid for directly, the customer requirements are similarly layered on top of the trust placed in your clinical and surgical skills. Over time, you and your staff may become enamored with the fact that you've performed hundreds or thousands of a particular procedure. Your practice may choose to use this as part of its marketing communications, signaling the tenure and experience you bring to the table. However, this makes it all too easy for you and your team to forget that while you may have done this thousands of times, it is likely the first and only time for your patient. It's a mental numbing that can lead to a less than enthusiastic encounter with the patient, which they will sense.

The trick is to keep things fresh for you and your staff. Maintaining this posture with each and every patient means that you are as excited as they are about the outcome you want to

achieve and the benefits it will provide for years to come. It does require conscious effort on your part to ensure that any unintentional cues, verbal or non-verbal, are avoided during the consultation, workup, or surgical encounters. On surgery day, the patient is likely in a heightened state with varying degrees of anxiety and excitement. Being on edge means they are also likely ultra-sensitive and will pick up on every word uttered and every action performed by you and your team, giving new meaning to that old adage, "Be on your best behavior." What's commonplace to you is new and unique to your patient. Keep this in mind as you go through your process so that it makes the patient feel special and important rather than part of the routine.

THIRTEEN

Giving the
Blessing

When a patient comes to see you, they are seeking your expertise and evaluation as to the appropriateness of a specific procedure. All too often, the physician abdicates this role by not making a specific recommendation and simply saying, "Here are your options, pick one." That type of response stems from a belief that it is not appropriate to sell or push patients and better to allow them to decide.

In the end, the patient will make a decision, but this thinking defeats the purpose of why they came to you in the first place. It's similar to going to the auto repair shop and being offered several mufflers to choose from after mechanics diagnosed the issue with your car. You likely have no idea which one is better and are counting on the mechanic's expertise to make the recommendation.

That patient is seeking your blessing during the consultation. The patient is experiencing multiple emotions simultaneously, ranging from hope (what will life be like after?) to fear (what if something goes wrong?). As the doctor, you are the person they are trusting to guide their decision and help them feel not just okay but confident in moving forward. This is a combination of the patient both being clinically qualified and having the right expectations, which are part of your responsibility in terms of diagnosis and recommendation (with emphasis here on setting realistic expectations and not over-promising). Get to know the patient's goals well enough so that you can make an appropriate recommendation to them with the objective of exceeding their expectations (a customer-centered approach).

If you are concerned about being viewed as a salesman by your patient, you should know the origin of the word itself. It's from the Scandinavian word Selzig, which means "to serve." The best salespeople aren't the stereotype of pushy or demanding but rather express care and concern to understand and meet the needs of their customers.

—FOURTEEN—

What Patients Remember

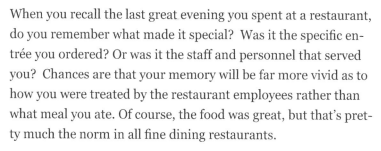

When you recall the last great evening you spent at a restaurant, do you remember what made it special? Was it the specific entrée you ordered? Or was it the staff and personnel that served you? Chances are that your memory will be far more vivid as to how you were treated by the restaurant employees rather than what meal you ate. Of course, the food was great, but that's pretty much the norm in all fine dining restaurants.

Restaurateur Danny Meyer understands that how a customer gets treated is far more memorable than what is actually served. "You feel better when you make other people feel good," Meyer explains in his book *Setting the Table*. Staff training in customer service focuses on developing one's HQ or Hospitality Quotient, which Meyer says is based on six emotional skills:

1. Being kind and optimistic, or having hope
2. Having an intellectual curiosity
3. Having a strong work ethic

4. Having empathy
5. Having self-awareness
6. Most importantly, having integrity

This approach to customer service explains why Meyer has been so successful. Many of his New York City restaurants (Gramercy Tavern, Union Square Café) rise to the top in ultra-competitive Manhattan. His most recent project, Shake Shack, is redefining the fast casual category and drawing huge crowds whenever a new location opens.

" PATIENTS REMEMBER HOW THEY WERE TREATED LONG AFTER THEY FORGET WHAT SERVICE YOU PERFORMED."

This same philosophy should be applied to your practice and affect how you interview and decide who to hire. Imagine how employees with these skills will fare when it comes to actively listening, addressing concerns, or going above and beyond when it comes to helping your patients. Indeed, those six emotional skills should be present in all customer-facing employees to ensure that you are building hospitality into your practice culture.

Just like fine-dining customers, patients remember how they were treated long after they forget what service you performed.

PEOPLE

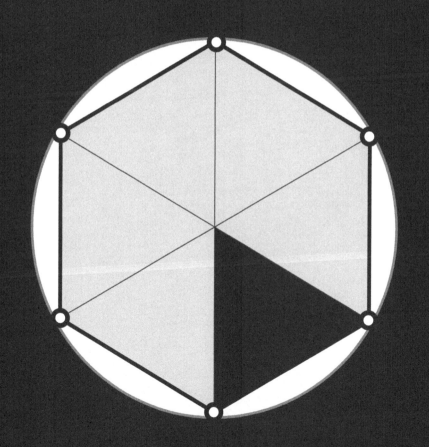

◈▶ PEOPLE

Most doctors I know are control freaks to some extent. If they could do every job in the practice, they would...if only to ensure tasks were completed to their exacting standards. But as you know, it takes a team to run a practice, often comprised of staff with varying degrees of experience, knowledge, and truth be told, passion to represent you and your practice. These insights are aimed to help you understand what it takes to attract and retain people that serve as an extension of you. As you will see, there's a lot to be learned from outside your practice that can greatly help you improve what you do inside your practice when it comes to the people you choose to be on your team.

Hire for Attitude

There is only one skill that cannot be trained, and that is attitude. Having a positive can-do attitude is the prerequisite for developing a service-responsive and servant-leadership mindset among all employees on the team. Because you as the doctor are the brand, you need to start choosing people who support that brand in all they do as employees in your practice.

When looking for new employees, it makes sense to look beyond the typical healthcare related job boards or recruiting firms. Some of the best new hires in medical practices have previous roles in hospitality, retail or customer service operations. Prior experience in restaurants, hotels, and retail stores offers skills that are more in tune with your practice's goals to become more customer-centric. These skills include active listening, problem solving, managing expectations and dealing with angry customers. When paired with a great attitude, these skills become competitive advantage for the practice as team members strive to fulfill the promise of the brand.

Additionally, you can seek to hire more seasoned employees looking for a second career following retirement. School teachers are typically excellent at patient education. A hotel's front desk receptionist can make a superb "Director of First Impressions" and bring a concierge-style approach to interacting with patients. Retail sales personnel can become outstanding counselors and schedulers. Restaurant managers have extensive training in operations and supervision.

These are the people you need on your team that can be counted on to build a practice culture that strives for top-notch customer service and a memorable patient experience. Given that healthcare is roughly one-fifth of our economy, you have the opportunity to attract great customer experience talent from other industries to your medical practice.

Among the questions you should ask is this one from Hyatt's Andaz hotel chain: "Do you enjoy entertaining people in your home?" The answer reveals a great deal about someone's attitude towards service. If patients are customers and you want to treat them like guests, then make sure you have the right people on the team with the right heart towards hospitality and service.

SIXTEEN

The Audition and the Bounty

An audition is something we associate with trying out for a play or, in places like Hollywood, getting cast in a movie or TV show. It's a good way for the director to figure out who's going to be the best fit for the prospective role. Bringing the concept of an audition to your practice is going to be equally valuable, if not more so, than a traditional job interview.

In a medical practice, having an audition means inviting prospective employees to spend a full day with your team, shadowing different employees throughout the day. Doing this (the candidate should be compensated for the time away from their current job) creates benefits for all involved. It allows the candidate to experience the culture of the practice in a direct way rather than just what they hear about from you or your administrator. It allows your team to be involved in the decision process for hiring, which boosts morale and loyalty to the practice. By the end of the day, both the candidate and your team should have a sense if the candidate is the right fit. This is one of the key steps in hiring used by customer service guru John DiJulius in his John Roberts Spa enterprise.

But the audition shouldn't end there. While a director's callbacks are designed to make sure they find the right person for the role, your audition should last throughout the first ninety days. This allows both parties to continue evaluating one another; the candidate is also auditioning you, making sure the workplace is a healthy and positive environment.

While hiring is an expensive and time-consuming process, a bad hiring decision is far more expensive. Nobody understands this better than Zappos' founder Tony Hsieh. Every new employee hired at this leading online retailer goes through four to six weeks of training and along the way gets exposed to their Ten Core Values, which include "Do More with Less" and "Create Fun and A Little Weirdness."

At the 2-week point in each training class, Tony Hsieh addresses the training class and concludes with a bounty, offering $2,000 to any employee willing to quit right then and there. This payment is in addition to the salary they've been collecting during training as a new hire. Up to 10% of the class take the money and leave. From Zappos' perspective, this is money well spent. It prevents the company from being infiltrated by less-than-committed employees. One of my physician clients instituted this for all employees regardless of tenure; he wanted to see if his longer-term employees shared his commitment to making the practice more customer-friendly.

Amazon, which acquired Zappos in 2009, similarly extended this idea to all their employees. Once a year, employees have the option of taking a $5,000 quitting bonus, with the condition that they can never work for the company again. CEO Jeff Bezos makes it clear he doesn't want employees to actually quit; he does want them to think about what they want. Employees re-up their commitment and are more engaged, according to the company. Very few actually take the money.

Having an audition is a far better way to evaluate potential employees. Offering a quitting bonus to help employees gracefully exit is a way to make sure you have the right people on the team to build your desired customer-focused culture.

ZAPPOS 10 CORE VALUES

1. Deliver WOW Through Service

2. Embrace and Drive Change

3. Create Fun and a Little Weirdness

4. Be Adventurous, Creative, and Open-Minded

5. Pursue Growth and Learning

6. Build Open and Honest Relationships With Communication

7. Build a Positive Team and Family Spirit

8. Do More with Less

9. Be Passionate and Determined

10. Be Humble

SEVENTEEN

Learning to KISS

A business principle that originated with the US Navy in 1960 was given the acronym KISS: Keep it simple, stupid. One area where practices struggle is in developing accurate job descriptions for each role in the practice. The same issue plagues many other businesses; just read any job description and it will have a list of responsibilities, followed by a catch-all statement such as "plus any other special projects or assignments as instructed by the manager." That statement likely does more harm than good as new employees fail to gain a clear definition of what they are responsible for at work.

Clothing retailer Nordstrom solved this problem by limiting their job description to four words: Serve and Be Kind. Those two actions sum up what the patient experience should be about. Additionally, Nordstrom has two basic job classifications: those who serve the customer directly and those who support them. Again, this serves as a way to keep things simple and also sets the tone that employees are going to need to have broader, more flexible skill sets so they can handle a wider range of duties and responsibilities.

Your medical practice can steal shamelessly from Nordstrom and put the KISS principle to work. The current list of jobs and roles can be classified into one of the two broad categories (serving the customer or supporting those who do). Specific roles and job titles can be converted into a list of tasks that need to be performed and then further subdivided by those tasks that require training or certification.

This reclassification can foster greater cooperation and team-work, as it can break down the walls that may have existed among different parts of the practice (clinical, surgical, back office) and allow for greater employee cross-training. As employees develop a broader set of skills, you are in a position to get the same amount of work accomplished with fewer employees overall. Each employee adds more value to your practice and the entire team should feel more capable as well as more valuable.

Keeping it simple and straightforward with job descriptions is definitely not stupid! It can be a great way to enhance the culture and make your practice an even better place to work.

EIGHTEEN

Building Your Culture

When discussing the importance of corporate culture in relation to corporate strategy, management expert Peter Drucker said it best: "Culture eats strategy for breakfast."

If you've never heard of Peter Drucker, it's worth spending some time reading his work, as he is widely considered the greatest business thought leader of all time. While culture may sound like something more appropriate for a corporation, it's role in your medical practice is no less important.

You can spend a lot of time and money on your strategy as well as your marketing plan, and if the people responsible for executing that strategy are not aligned and enthusiastically supporting team goals, you will fail to achieve them. This is part of the reason why the organizational culture within your practice is far more critical to your success than any grandiose plans. Perhaps the bigger reason is that given how much of your life is spent at work, it should be a place where you and your team actually look forward to spending time together.

Building a great practice culture is easy to say and hard to do. It takes a daily commitment that is on par with your clinical care, as culture impacts people and how they do what they do as members of your team. You know who your all-star "A Team" players are in your practice; they are the ones who have a can-do attitude and whom you can rely on to get things done no matter what. You also know who your sub-par B players are in the practice; they are the ones who show up but don't have the level of effort or commitment that you expect. They do the bare minimum, just enough to get by. And that's the problem. Your tolerance of mediocre performance is like a death blow to building a great culture, as the B players' very existence on the team sends a message to the A Team players that it's okay not to work so hard. This message spreads like a cancer and infects others in the organization: "Why should I work so hard if there's no difference between the value of my effort and that of others who don't try as hard?" This is a fair question to ask. How you answer it as a leader impacts the culture of the practice.

" BUILDING A GREAT PRACTICE CULTURE IS EASY TO SAY AND HARD TO DO. IT TAKES A DAILY COMMITMENT THAT IS ON PAR WITH YOUR CLINICAL CARE"

Further, most B players view themselves incorrectly. They believe they are A Team material, often suffering from low self awareness coupled with a sense of entitlement. This combination can be explosive, especially since this type of person tends to be defensive when confronted. It's not entirely their fault, as their behavior has been tolerated and rationalized over time. For instance, the reasoning may be something like, "She's been here for over twenty years" or "We can't get rid of him; patients love him."

If you want a great culture that can withstand all the pressures that come with working in a medical environment, you need to make sure you stack your team with A players and become brave enough to confront B players if behavior and attitude doesn't change, removing them if necessary. Remember, the A Team is counting on you!

Beyond Bedside Manner

NINETEEN

The Director of First Impressions

You know that person you hired for $15 an hour to be your receptionist? He or she has far more impact on your practice than you realize. That person you've entrusted to the front desk and likely the telephone is more aptly titled your Director of First Impressions.

You've probably heard the phrase "You don't get a second chance to make a first impression," which instinctively recalls key moments in your life – a job interview, that first date – where the first impression mattered. A lot.

It's no different at your practice with the first impression you make (intended or not) on patients. The human brain works very quickly, forming impressions in milliseconds. And what patients experience when they first walk into your practice informs how they think about you even before they ever shake your hand.

Upon the arrival of each patient, the most critical assignment is given to your front office person. Far more than a receptionist, they are the quarterback who leads the play on the field when someone arrives. As a Director of First Impressions, they need to take charge of what happens once the door opens.

There are three key areas of focus for this role. First is the environment- making sure it is clean and pristine. Second is what is known as "the greet," which is comprised of the welcoming words first spoken that will set the tone for the entire visit. And third is a well-defined hospitality step, which should include an offer of refreshments and a quick check to see if the newly arrived guest has any immediate needs such as a restroom or a WiFi connection.

From there, the Director should provide clear communication about what will take place next and set proper expectations. Much of this can be garnered on the spot by looking at the type of appointment as well as knowing how things are flowing in the clinic. If there's going to be a delay, let the patient know. If there's not enough time to have a cup of coffee because the nurse or technician is taking them straight back, let the patient know.

The importance of this role cannot be overstated. Practices tend to put the least experienced, least knowledgeable, and least compensated employees in this role. That's a big mistake when the goal is to create an experience that is unique and memorable. Think about places you've visited where the service was wonderful; the venue didn't try to cut corners during those critical first moments. Instead, it has a well-trained host or similar welcomer that gets things started off on the right foot. It's time your practice did the same.

Beyond Bedside Manner

TWENTY

The Calling Card

The origin of the business card dates back to 15th century China, where people would carry around "visiting cards" to impress those they wished to meet. In 17th century Europe, slightly larger "trade cards" were used to make it easier for people to find businesses and often included a map on one side. As the industrial revolution got underway, the lines between social and trade interaction came together, leading to today's "business card" being used to introduce ourselves during an initial meeting.

There's talk these days about the business card going the way of the Dodo Bird, headed towards extinction as we share contact information digitally rather than by handing over a card.

That talk should be ignored and the opposite – providing a business card to each and every employee at the practice – should be the norm.

This is one of those easy wins for a practice, yet it's surprising how few put this insight to work. A box of five hundred business cards costs about $20, a modest investment when one starts to imagine the potential gains. The inhibiting factor is more likely cultural, stemming from a lack of awareness of this tactic but potentially also rooted in a misunderstanding regarding the value of each employee as a source of new patients.

" EACH AND EVERY EMPLOYEE HAS THE POTENTIAL TO BE AN AMBASSADOR FOR THE PRACTICE; THE RETURN ON THAT INVESTMENT IS ESSENTIALLY INFINITE"

When given the opportunity, medical practice employees want to talk about where they work and the impact it has on lives. They tend to take pride in their role, regardless of the stress or pressure of the daily schedule, especially if you've established what business you're in, invested in your brand, and focused on improving your culture. By providing each person a card with their name and contact information on it as a representative of your practice, you can do wonders for their own self-image and cultivate their sense of ownership in the success of the practice.

Once armed with their own business cards, employees should be able to hand them out freely, encouraging patients to contact them with any questions. When properly trained, they expand and extend your influence to help your patients live better lives.

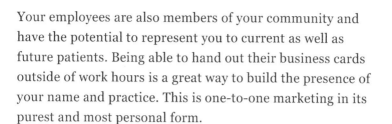

Your employees are also members of your community and have the potential to represent you to current as well as future patients. Being able to hand out their business cards outside of work hours is a great way to build the presence of your name and practice. This is one-to-one marketing in its purest and most personal form.

Each and every employee has the potential to be an ambassador for the practice; the return on that investment is essentially infinite, both in the potential for new patients and, more immediately, in the increase in satisfaction and loyalty among your employees who have a tangible reminder, "I'm part of something special."

It's more than a business card. It's a calling card.

TWENTY-ONE

Concierge Training

With so much emphasis on credentialing for doctors and staff, you would think that certification would extend beyond clinical care into the realm of customer service. It has not.

For the practice that is serious and committed to customer excellence, ongoing training must be part of the development plan for employees. Otherwise, it's just not reasonable to expect that employees will be able to carry out protocols or processes designed to delight the customer when patients are at your practice.

One of the best ways to jumpstart such training is to enlist the services of a local hotel concierge. They have specialized training in dealing with all sorts of customers and all sorts of requests as well as complaints. They tend to be as patient as they are knowledgeable in guiding hotel guests with recommendations, directions or connections to additional resources that will benefit the guest's overall experience. The core of these skills – listening, serving and problem solving – are at the heart of what it is required by your team members to become excellent at customer service.

You would be wise to close down the office for an afternoon and hire a concierge to do a workshop for your practice. Just like most of your staff, concierges tend to be on the "front line" with customers and are able to quickly command attention and admiration from your team members. A good concierge will be able to relate to the issues your staff faces in terms of pleasing patients' needs. They will also bring an expert problem-solving mentality to your practice that may have kinda/sorta been there but not formally codified and made part of the practice culture.

One illustration of this comes from Vance Thompson Vision in South Dakota. A technician overheard a patient say how much he enjoyed the hot and sour soup at a local Chinese restaurant whenever he came to Sioux Falls. This elderly gentleman had traveled several hours from his home and was being prepped for cataract surgery. Later in the recovery area following the procedure, a bowl of his favorite soup from that restaurant was waiting for him. Imagine his surprise! The technician did not ask permission (or even ask to be reimbursed). She just did what she had been trained to do, delighting the customer in a practice culture that encourages this type of engagement.

Imagine a team where every employee takes a concierge approach to each and every encounter: Your patients will notice, and those encounters will lead to stories, some of which will be experiences that go well above and beyond what is expected in a medical practice. Those stories become part of your culture and part of the practice legend. They get shared and build your reputation in ways that advertising cannot.

TWENTY-TWO

Job-Career-Calling

Boutique hotelier Chip Conley was known for instituting a unique theme at each of his properties in northern California. His design methodology was to create a hotel experience that would appeal to a specific demographic segment, which typically resembled the readers of the magazine. This was really clever as a marketing approach. "In an industry where every location is essentially a box-shaped building, you have to take a different approach to differentiate your offering" he once told me.

His very first, the Phoenix Hotel, was located in a less desirable part of San Francisco, yet became popular among touring rock bands with its Rolling Stone magazine theme. He was extremely proud of the three thousand plus employees spread out across twenty hotels, "half of whom clean toilets for a living." His lessons on management and leadership have become role models for an industry where turnover rate ranges between 75% to 100% (meaning that an entire hotel staff could change every twelve to sixteen months).

Chip Conley did more than theme his hotels; he gave a lot of thought and effort to how each employee could find deep meaning in their work, no matter their role. In fact, he decided that his employees were just as important as customers and shareholders, and that if he created the right culture, his hotels could generate profits that were sustainable (i.e., without the need to advertise) and higher than industry averages. He was the rare hotel executive who understood that developing a strong culture with the right values would lead to more loyal customers. In the hospitality industry, he created competitive advantage by empowering his employees with the knowledge and training to serve customers better than other hotels would.

He engaged an entire hotel's staff in offsites, educating them and then asking employees—including, bartenders, housekeepers, and front desk staff – to come up with a strategy for their hotel. His view was that by providing service employees with a sense of calling, this would lead to higher employee satisfaction and better overall experience for guests. It worked. Employee satisfaction scores were off the charts and the employee turnover rate during the 2001 recession was in the 20-30% range, far lower than the rest of the industry.

Conley documented much of this success in his book *PEAK!*, which puts a twist on Maslow's hierarchy of needs by applying it to work. His hierarchy of Job-Career-Calling serves as a good framework to hire and develop employees in your practice.

At the base of the pyramid is the view that work is a job that offers a paycheck in exchange for performing work. The next level up is when the role is viewed as a career, with the employee feeling like they could stay and grow in the practice for years to come. And at the top is when the employee sees their role as

Beyond Bedside Manner

their calling, the fit between what they have to offer (passion, skill) and what you as their employer can do to help them fully realize their gifts. This leads to a work environment for that person that is far beyond having a job.

Your role as leader of the practice is to identify and attract more team members who view their job as their calling.

THE EMPLOYEE PYRAMID

TWENTY-THREE

Lead and Be Led

Strong leadership as a trait and a skill has been studied throughout the ages. We all know great leadership when we see it, and much of what makes a leader great is their ability to communicate effectively. Similarly, communication is at the heart of what makes a practice great. Sometimes it's helpful to take a step back and understand why. It is the glue that holds people accountable so that as a team they can perform their duties on behalf of patients and one another. When it comes to how you communicate internally, there are hundreds of resources available, with courses, systems, and consultants all available to help your practice collectively improve this vital skill.

What many doctors find helpful is the distinction between the two styles of communication: authoritarian and authoritative. Although they are separated by only a few letters, these two words convey completely different meanings when it comes to how you communicate and interact with your staff. Being authoritarian has its place, especially in the operating room where your orders must be followed, as any deviation can mean the difference between success or failure in surgery or even the difference between life and death.

Outside the operating room, you want to be authoritative. In contrast with the top-down, command and control style of the authoritarian leader, being authoritative involves being warm, nurturing and willing to listen. It's a style that still sets boundaries and limits and includes taking action to make sure staff members complete tasks in their respective areas of responsibility.

Being authoritative typically gains you much more ground in terms of earning the respect and admiration of your staff. Knowing that they are listened to and their opinions valued, they will respond with greater productivity and loyalty. This style of leadership shows that you have faith in your team and opens the door for another style known as servant leadership. The servant leader's role is to support the development and success of each direct report in achieving the organization's objectives. It's a literal "turn on its head" organization chart that has the CEO at the bottom and everyone else above. Employees at all levels possess leadership skills and the servant leader wants them to be put to work for the good of the organization. For a medical practice, this means leadership gets exhibited in ways that meaningfully improve the patient experience.

While medical school ingrained how to be an autocratic leader with an authoritarian style of communication, succeeding in leading your medical practice requires a distinct authoritative approach. These three guiding principles will help you develop the authoritative style that your staff wants to see in their leader:

First, over-communicate.

Do not be afraid to repeat what you want for your practice. Be detailed and use analogies and examples from outside of the office to help people understand. Your team will want to hear it multiple times and it will take time and repetition for it to sink in.

Second, set expectations.

With your goals and objectives in mind, clearly define expectations for yourself and for each and every member of your team. These expectations need to become the norm within your practice culture.

Third, train continuously.

Too many doctors think of training as an event that happens periodically. On the contrary, training is critical and should happen continuously. Training is key because it teaches and reinforces your goals and expectations. Continuous training is a key part of how you communicate your vision and values.

Communicate the expectations that you set and be willing to continuously train. This is what it means to be an authoritative leader as you develop your team so that together you achieve the goals and vision for your practice. There is no shortcut.

" COMMUNICATE THE EXPECTATIONS THAT YOU SET AND BE WILLING TO CONTINUOUSLY TRAIN."

PLACE

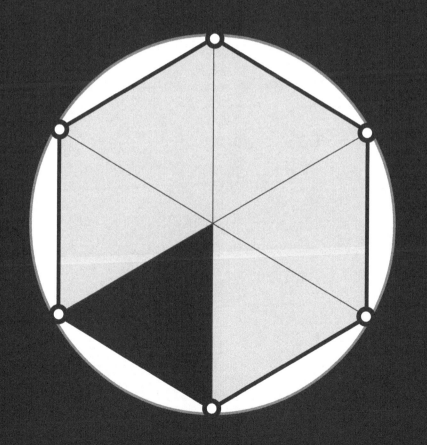

PLACE

Your practice is the place where things happen. You think of it as your office or medical practice or clinic. As the physical location where you and your team interact with patients, it is a place where you have the power and ability to design and control what occurs. This section of insights covers the two biggest elements of your place: the environment you create, and the experience guided by staff behavior. Along with the direct interaction you have with patients, the environment and behavior of your team have the greatest impact on the experience your patients have as customers in your practice.

—TWENTY-FOUR—

It's About Time

As with every business today, your desire to attract more consumers to become patients in your practice requires you to think differently about what it is they value as customers. It is no longer just about the services you perform; it is now about how the customer values the time spent with you.

People increasingly strive to save money on goods and services so they can spend more of their time and money on experiences.

Take escape rooms, an offering that didn't even exist in 2010. A decade later, there are over ten thousand of them. From rage rooms to axe-throwing lounges, TopGolf to Meow Wolf, places like these are attracting consumers in droves because they are highly engaging and compelling experiences. The latest edition of *The Experience Economy* introduces a new metric called The Money Value of Time, where value can be measured in terms of cost per minute to the customer. A two-

" TIME IS THE NEW MONEY."

hour movie runs about ten cents a minute. A round of golf at Pebble Beach costs two dollars a minute. The metric provides a new way to measure your business by putting money in the context of time spent.

From a healthcare perspective, a visit to the doctor was meant to be efficient and focused on time saved. Get 'em in, get 'em out. See as many patients as possible, especially as reimbursements decline. Efficiency was seen as the best way to optimize revenue and income (i.e., money). This was good for the doctor but not so good for the patient, especially if the patient was forced to wait a long time before or in the middle of appointments.

The Experience Economy turns this notion on its head. Less time spent creates a path to commoditization and less value. You are now competing for the time and attention of consumers as well as their wallet, and you need to think differently about the role time plays in your offering.

Time is the New Money.

You want the patient to view the experience as time well spent. Achieving this takes more work on your part to plan the overall experience so that it delights the customer. This means eliminating the routine violations that occur when you ask patients to fill out forms when they arrive. This should have been done beforehand. Or when patients are meant to wait with nothing to do. These are two among many examples of time that is wasted.

Concierge medicine illustrates what is possible in a medical practice. Originally perceived as catering to wealthy patients,

115

this practice model has gone mainstream and attracted corporate franchises. Doctors charge a monthly fee that patients pay in order to get more access and more time with their physician. Concierge offerings are rising in popularity and not just because the traditional healthcare model is broken. Patients are viewing their allocation of time – the one resource that no one can make more of – with increasing scrutiny.

Are your customers spending more or less time with you? If the answer is less, then you need to re-examine what you are doing as you are on the path towards commoditization of the services you offer. By engaging your patients in ways that they find to be personal and meaningful, you can move in the other direction. Customization of the experience serves as the antidote to commoditization. It means more time that is well spent and ultimately greater value for you and your patients.

TWENTY-FIVE

Clean the House

Before you have guests come over to your home, you make sure the house is clean and everything is prepared. Everything should be in order. But this principle is routinely violated in medical practices, especially by those who invest in paid marketing to attract new patients.

The problem is that your patients as "guests" are typically invited to come over before the house is clean and ready for a warm welcome. They arrive and often find your front entry a mess and don't receive an enthusiastic greeting. The host's nowhere near ready as everything's running behind schedule. These are examples of the wrong impression and don't make your practice more attractive. Some basic rules of hospitality have been violated.

Sadly, this scenario happens all the time and can be illustrated by the way most practices answer the telephone. In studies conducted by our firm to assess phone inquiries from prospective LASIK patients, only 29% of practices achieved what was set as a reasonable standard that would motivate a patient to schedule a consultation. Recordings of the conversations (done with permission) revealed a lack of subject knowledge as well as reasonable telephone skills. These studies demonstrate that the house is still messy and money spent on advertising is premature. Although leads are generated, they end up not being handled effectively and the patient chooses either not to have the procedure or to go somewhere else.

The problem does not go away for prospective patients visiting the practice. They're often greeted poorly and asked to sit in a waiting room before being taken back. Tests are done, consultations are performed, recommendations are made... only to have the patient conclude that they "need to think about it," a polite way of saying no.

While there is a lot of work that can be done to build a practice before it turns to paying for advertising, the key insight here is to learn how to live by the Golden Rule of hospitality in your practice. Assign a staff member, typically the receptionist, to serve in a greater welcoming capacity - just like when a guest arrives at your home. Major businesses know how to do this; Walmart has Greeters and Delta Airlines has Redcoats. Their role is to make people feel welcome and appreciated. That should be the goal of your practice as you greet patients and recognize they are also your customers.

TWENTY-SIX

The Platinum Rule

We've all heard the Golden Rule, which goes something like "Treat others the way you wish to be treated." While it was popularized by Jesus as the 2nd Great Commandment, its origins trace back to early hunter-gatherers around 10,000 BC, who found that cooperative hunting works better than everyone only working to save themselves.

This seems reasonable for the medical practice until one recognizes the flaw in the Golden Rule when it comes to how we treat patients. It's time for an upgrade, says author and colleague Dave Kerpen, who preaches the Platinum Rule in his book *The Art of People.*

He points out that while the Golden Rule is simple, it doesn't take into account that everyone is different. "The truth is that in many cases what you'd want done to you is different from what your partner, employee, customer, investor, wife or child would want done to him or her," he said in an interview with Inc. Magazine.

Here's the Platinum Rule: Do unto others as they would want done to them.

Still simple. Yet far more powerful, especially as it relates to the concept of personalization and customization of the patient experience.

In his book, Kerpen quotes a story that Dale Carnegie told which illustrates the Platinum Rule:

Personally I am very fond of strawberries and cream, but I have found that for some strange reason, fish prefer worms. So when I went fishing, I didn't think about what I wanted. I thought about what they wanted. I didn't bait the hook with strawberries and cream. Rather, I dangled a worm or grasshopper in front of the fish and said: "Wouldn't you like to have that?"

In a medical practice, this means taking time to understand what the patient's goals are before making a recommendation that you would like yourself. This is not to be confused with "If you were my relative, this is what I'd recommend you do." Rather, take a brief moment to imagine what life is like for that person you are counseling and tailor your recommendation so that it is designed and described as "one and only" and applies only to him or her. In short, make it about them and not about you.

It's time to upgrade to Platinum when it comes to how you treat people in your practice.

Blow Up the Waiting Room

Think about your own experiences interacting with businesses, especially those that you visit in person. You may observe how you are greeted and how long it takes to be served or have your needs addressed. Most businesses that deal with customers invest in creating a welcoming environment both through their people and their physical space.

In medicine, we tend to do the opposite. Most doctors' offices pay little attention to the greeting beyond a cursory hello and then ask people to wait...in a space called a "waiting room." The name itself seems antiquated in a society that is starved for time and hates to wait for anything. Smartphones only hasten this, as information is instantly accessible from the palm of your hand.

The descriptor "waiting room" is another negative cue in the experience and, perhaps more than any other aspect of the visit to a doctor's office, is begging for change. Here are some of the questions that go on in people's minds while they are waiting:

When are they going to call me back?

What is taking so long?

Why did they take that person back who arrived after me?

Where did they find these uncomfortable seats?

Who is in charge?

The longer they have to wait, the more irritated they become. The more irritated they become, the more likely it will negatively impact the overall experience. And although they may not express it to you as the doctor, they may well take their displeasure out on the staff or, increasingly common, complain about it to others. Online review sites make it easy and convenient for frustrated customers to voice their frustration.

This fixture of the medical office needs to be eliminated immediately. Indeed, it's time to blow up the waiting room (figuratively speaking, of course).

When speaking to physician audiences, I'll often ask for a quick show of hands as to how many still routinely use the term "waiting room" as part of their language. Typically more than half will admit they do. I notice many of them begin jotting down ideas for new names.

Reception area, front room, welcome center—these are some of the more effective names people have come up with to describe the space.

If you have worked to develop a theme for your practice's environment and have designed the space accordingly, then the name of the room can be more specialized to reflect the theme: gallery (art), on deck circle (sports), green room (entertainment).

And while it's important to change the name of the room, it's even more important to change its function. Rather than simply make people wait, rethink what can take place in that room prior to patients being brought back to start the exam or consultation. The days of having a pile of magazines, many of which are old and worn, are no longer adequate. What is essential is that when people are required to wait, you have a variety of options in place to change the dynamic of waiting. Keep in mind the following formula:

Waiting + Activity = Activity

When you mix in another activity with waiting, what people recall is that their time was spent doing that activity rather than waiting.

As you reimagine what can and should occur in that place formerly known as a place to wait, here are some ideas to help you use that waiting time to educate, entertain, or refresh those who have arrived at your practice. They are meant to get you started on your "demolition" project:

Install a flat screen television with visually stimulating programming (e.g., Planet Earth); avoid television programming that is anxiety-inducing (e.g., local or cable news, financial).

Have a computer station with internet access so people can check e-mail.

Provide WiFi access so that people can get on the internet on their own laptop computers. Use the "guest" functionality on every router so you don't have to worry about someone hacking your network.

Purchase several hand-held devices such as iPads (older generations of which can be bought for a song) and portable DVD players (under $100) that can be used for education on your practice or your services.

Create a library of DVDs available with popular TV shows and movies for use with those portable DVD players. Alternatively, have a Netflix account that people can access and then watch just about whatever they want.

Invest in a brochure designed specifically for your practice: "Twenty reasons why our practice is the place for you" will allow people to get a better understanding of all the services you offer, your core values, and other facts that distinguish and differentiate your practice.

If your patient is arriving to discuss a particular service or procedure, use that initial time to have them learn about that procedure through specific literature, DVD or even a website.

Offer a library of paperback books that patients can donate to as well as use for pleasure reading. This extends your reading selection beyond the typical rack of magazines. It's your in-office version of the Free Tiny Library movement springing up in communities everywhere.

Provide refreshments that are dedicated to patients and family members and offered upon arrival. Think beyond a water cooler and a pot of coffee to what would be perceived as nice hospitality. Tea conveys soothing and calm, fresh fruit symbolizes health and vitality, and freshly baked cookies suggest warmth and home.

Whatever you choose to do, get your team involved in the process. The first room that patients enter when they arrive deserves to set the tone for the exceptional experience and care that you strive to provide.

TWENTY-EIGHT

Avoid Identity Theft

When we hear about identity theft, we immediately think about the bad things that happen when someone's credit cards have been stolen or bank accounts have been hacked. Yet there's another form of identity theft that, while not financially lethal, takes place millions of times each day in medical practices. This is the inability of a practice to properly identify patients, not for HIPAA but rather for the common courtesy and respect it conveys when somebody knows you by your name without having to be asked.

Much like the TV sitcom *Cheers*, your patients want to come to your practice knowing that "everybody knows their name."

This can be accomplished at two different moments before the appointment even begins. It involves using a simple but effective technology to create a more personable experience: the sticky note.

When the patient arrives, your Director of First Impressions makes a note of what that patient is wearing and places that note on the chart. When the practice is ready to bring the patient back, the technician or nurse scans the reception area to find that person. Instead of calling out their name from the doorway (highly impersonal as well as a potential HIPAA violation!), the staff member walks up to the patient, gives a personal greeting and takes them back to continue the visit. This brief act,which costs nothing, can have a huge impact on the patient's perception of being cared for, can be easily trained, and does not require additional equipment.

The other opportunity is a bit more advanced as a means of patient identification. Take a picture and incorporate it into the electronic medical record or practice management software. This will allow you to identify and greet each patient by name as they reach the front desk. This act will surprise and likely delight: "They know me, they remember me."

By preserving your patient's identity when they arrive at your practice, you take advantage of an easy opportunity to make them feel special and important. Don't miss it!

TWENTY-NINE

Lights! Camera! Action!

Whether on a movie set or a Broadway stage, there is a moment when the curtain goes up, the camera starts rolling, and the action begins.

The same thing takes place each day when your practice opens its doors. You are immediately on stage, so to speak. *The Experience Economy* authors Pine and Gilmore emphasize this with the subtitle of the first edition of the book: "Work is Theater and Every Business a Stage."

The point here is that in the eyes of your customer, they are the audience to a performance put on by you and your staff. In an earlier insight we explored how the hiring process should function like an audition — hopefully you held successful auditions and rehearsals because now that the patients are here, it's showtime!

When you go to a play or a movie, you have certain expectations about how the performance will unfold. Your patients are no different when they come to see you. For example, they expect the show – in this context, their appointment - to start on time. From this point forward, think about your physical office as having two distinct environments; the one that patients experience (see, hear, feel) can be thought of as "on stage." And the one they should never experience is what we call "backstage."

Having a backstage is critical because employees need a place where their conversations and actions are not a part of the performance. All too often this space is not set apart, and a boundary is crossed where patients get exposed to something that isn't meant to be part of the experience. A common violation is banter or talk among the staff that can be overheard by patients, which signals that they are not the focus of the moment. When this banter includes what happened on last night's date, the message sent to the patient is "They're too busy to get on with my appointment but not too busy to gossip." It's disrespectful and a clear negative cue in the overall experience.

" HAVING A BACKSTAGE IS CRITICAL BECAUSE EMPLOYEES NEED A PLACE WHERE THEIR CONVERSATIONS AND ACTIONS ARE NOT A PART OF THE PERFORMANCE."

This type of chatter should never take place on stage. You wouldn't expect two actors in the middle of a performance to break out of character and start discussing last night's ball game.

That would be a clear violation of their role. It's the same for you and your staff.

As the doctor, you are the star of the show. Be mindful so as to live up to (and exceed) the expectations of your audience in your leading role. From an acting perspective, the diagnostic tests and workup conducted by your technicians or nurses are props which allow you to perform in your starring role. Putting this all together - stage, supporting cast, and props - should be designed to make you look good and to have the patient walk away after the performance thinking "That was great," independent of the clinical outcome.

Make no mistake, acting is not to be confused with being fake or inauthentic. On the contrary, knowing your role and having your lines memorized is what you already do. Just like great actors and actresses, putting your heart into each and every patient encounter, even if you've said the same line thousands of times, is what it takes to be a star in the mind of your patients.

Beyond Bedside Manner

Engaging the Senses

One of the key opportunities to enhance customer experience is to more fully engage the senses. Traditionally, medical practices have only been concerned with what people see or where people sit. During a renovation or redecoration, most of the attention is paid to what will go on the wall (color, art, signage) and perhaps some new furnishings.

Practices should take a broader view and think about how they might enhance not only sight and touch but also what people hear, smell and, figuratively speaking, taste.

A method to do this in your practice, courtesy of Pine and Gilmore, is a Sensory Assessment of different places within your practice. The exercise is easy to do and can involve many members of the team. Pick one room to start and expand to more with time and experience. As you will see shortly, each place you assess will identify a long list of "room for improvement" items.

A good place to start is the reception area. Restrooms, a diagnostic testing area or secondary waiting area are also good candidates for assessment.

The assessment team should be instructed to record their observations, on each of the following:

What do I see?

What do I hear?

What do I smell?

What do I touch?

Given that taste is the least refined of our senses, the observational technique becomes,

What sense of taste is evoked?

By spending a minute on each, quickly and quietly working alone with their own recording device (pen and paper or Notes app on the iPhone), the team can quickly generate a large list of observations, which can then be shared in a group discussion.

The goal here is primarily to identify what Pine and Gilmore termed negative cues in the environment. Anything that detracts from the level of service and overall experience you intend for your patients is considered a negative cue. In my consulting experience, it is better to start with negative cues that you should eliminate before implementing positive cues that can be deployed to enhance the experience. While the first question on sight will likely uncover flaws that remained invisible prior to the exercise (stained carpets, torn wallpaper), the remaining senses should also be equally explored.

Sound is particularly important and can be influenced by eliminating staff chatter (which should be reserved for backstage) and possibly adding music.

Touch can refer to any surface that is touched by a staff member or customer, paying attention to both cleanliness (when was the last time certain areas were dusted?) and comfort (how does this chair material feel?).

The way a practice smells is also ripe for opportunity. More and more practices are using nice scents in different rooms that evoke calmness and tranquility.

And the sense of taste can also relate to how your practice is perceived. Ask yourself what sense of taste is evoked as you walk through your practice. At one end is mint (suggesting fresh and clean), while on the negative end would be burnt coffee (suggesting stale or old).

You will likely be surprised at how many observations are generated. The exercise can be a great team-building experience and help motivate additional ideas from your employees to further enhance the customer experience.

Once you've eliminated negative cues and banished them forevermore, the follow-up effort can extend to an overall makeover of the practice (extreme or not) to institute layout, design and behavior that comprise positive cues to your patients.

As previously mentioned, first impressions are everything, so think of each of the five senses as an opportunity to create a sensory impression. These are often small and subtle insertions that represent different colors used to paint the perfect picture of your practice for first time visitors as well as regular patients. This is an opportunity to brighten your patient's day and boost their spirits even before they are greeted by your Director of First Impressions. Engaging all the senses is yet another detail-oriented approach to differentiating your practice.

THIRTY-ONE

Customer Protocols

From the time you were a first-year resident, you were trained to deliver great care and achieve the best clinical outcomes possible for your patients. Once in private practice, you implemented protocols to make sure you and your staff were consistent in how you wanted patient history taken and tests performed. In the operating room, you put surgical protocols in place to refine technique and achieve superior surgical outcomes. Most surgeons maintain this mindset throughout their career, never ceasing to evaluate and adopt a technology or a process that will improve results.

Similar to your protocols, most successful businesses have dissected their operations to define each touchpoint with the customer, set a standard for what should take place, and determine what to do if something goes wrong. The CEO of SAS Airlines understands this well, saying his employees have five million opportunities each day to make a positive impression.

The simple math is they average one million fliers a day, each of which typically has five interactions with his employees (check-in, gate, boarding, flight attendants and the pilot).

You have the opportunity to apply that same thinking to the customer-side of your practice. There are multiple interactions taking place before and after the patient spends time with you. Developing standards for each and every one of them helps everyone on the team understand the difference between what is acceptable and what falls short. Things will go wrong, and when a failure of service occurs, all the members of your team need to know how to handle the situation.

Taking the customer side of your practice as seriously as the clinical side requires a strong commitment and daily effort. Achieving excellence on a consistent basis is much easier said than done. Once you gain momentum in this area, you will likely be surprised at the response of both your team as well as your patients. It will take time to overcome initial skepticism, but once you do, your practice will be well positioned to consistently achieve a high standard of customer service. This will go far building value in the mind of your customer, as it is both difficult to consistently achieve and next to impossible for another practice to copy.

TOUCHPOINTS

CLINICAL	CUSTOMER
Intake (Patient History)	Greeting upon arrival
Diagnostic Testing	On-time appointments
Clinical Evaluation	Taking patients back to begin appointment
Pre-Surgical Preparation	Technician/Nurse interaction
Surgical Steps and Processes	Uncovering patient goals (doctor and counselor)
Post-Surgical Follow-Up	Escort, Farewell and Next Steps

THIRTY-TWO

The Daily Huddle

Having a successful and thriving medical practice takes communication and teamwork. This seems obvious, but many practices fail to create and sustain infrastructure that allows for solid communication on a regular basis.

Monthly or even weekly staff meetings, while able to cover some issues, are too far removed from the activities taking place every workday. Posting a daily schedule for staff to see when they walk in is helpful but isn't interactive.

A better way to address the busyness of the day is to have a daily huddle each morning, with all staff expected to attend.

These should last five to ten minutes and provide a way to get the team to focus on that day: who's coming in, any special needs, staff birthdays or anniversaries, emerging issues that negatively impact the patient experience. The agenda should also be used to recognize team members who do something great in the practice or receive kudos from a patient.

Having a huddle each morning will energize you and your staff and set a positive tone that can carry on throughout the day. Different staff members can be assigned to lead the huddle; it doesn't need to be the practice manager or supervisor. Employees can participate by preparing a brief inspirational story or quote to share.

The main goal is that the daily huddle becomes a daily habit of checking-in and reestablishing connections among the staff and the values of your practice. It is an event that should not be sacrificed, even if some members cannot attend on a given day.

Once established, many will look forward to this morning ritual. Others may resist at first, eventually coming along because they see the positive impact on the staff and the practice culture. A stubborn few may yet remain cynical; they are not worth the time or effort to convince otherwise. These employees typically leave when they realize the practice is changing and not returning to its old self.

Remember, the customer experience for your patients is highly dependent on your employees. The employee experience is what will make or break how patients perceive the practice. Every opportunity to enhance communication serves as a means of building trusting relationships and changing the culture of the practice for the better.

THIRTY-THREE

Avoid the Over-Under

When we talk about patient satisfaction, there is a singular bad habit among doctors which can be thought of as the over-under. In an effort to alleviate patients' concerns about a procedure, doctors over-promise results. This creates a risk of under-delivering and ultimately disappointing the client. As boutique hotelier Chip Conley puts it, "Disappointment is the result of poorly managed expectations."

Getting rid of this over-under instinct involves redefining patient satisfaction and learning a new method for setting expectations. Doctors who measure patient satisfaction often look no further than the results of their procedure. This traditional view focuses solely on the outcome as an absolute metric. But that is not how a patient's mind works, especially from a customer perspective. A procedure could go well surgically speaking and still leave the patient dissatisfied. Ultimately, success in surgery begins with how you discuss the procedure and set expectations beforehand. This is followed by how well you treat them after the procedure and during the follow-up period. Surgery - especially if it is elective - is a highly considered, emotional decision, and patient satisfaction is influenced by more than just the clinical outcome.

Patient satisfaction should be managed so that you maximize the number of satisfied patients and minimize the number of times someone is not pleased with their outcome. A simple acronym will help you remember to do this: UPOD. Under-promise and over-deliver. This is far better than its opposite, where you over-promise and under-deliver.

UPOD is all about the expectations you set with your patient regarding pain, recovery and outcome. It's no different than what happens when you are still at the office and your spouse is working to get dinner on the table. If you say you'll be home at six pm and walk in the door ten minutes early, you are a hero. But arrive ten minutes late, you look bad, the food's getting cold, and everybody at home is grumpy rather than excited to see you.

Be a hero. Under-promising gives you the ability to over-deliver relative to the expectations held by your customer.

THIRTY-FOUR

The Role
of Technology

In recent years, many grocery stores added automated check-out lanes. Their hypothesis was that customers would prefer the convenience of self-checkout rather than having to wait in line for a checker and bagger. Financially speaking, they saw an opportunity to replace human labor with a machine and achieve cost savings by shifting labor to the customer. Many of us, myself included, initially liked the opportunity to get out of the store faster. But the problems mounted, including malfunctioning scanners (which require human intervention to fix), operator error (when I can't seem to find the code for bananas), and the computer voice that seems annoyed when I make a mistake. For me and probably a lot of people, the service got worse and negatively impacted the shopping experience.

So much of our traditional face-to-face interaction has been eliminated in the past twenty years (about 85%, according to John DiJulius) that I actually appreciate that moment of chit-chat with the checkout clerk at the store. It seems that some of the larger grocery chains feel the same way and have chosen to add more checkers and even remove self-checkout lanes entirely. This is just one example of how technology and automation threaten the opportunity to improve service or enhance the experience.

" TECHNOLOGY SHOULD ONLY BE ADDED IF IT SERVES TO ENHANCE THE CUSTOMER EXPERIENCE."

Although medical technology is intended to make life easier, it is often wielded as a double-edged sword. When it comes to clinical diagnosis and surgical treatment, innovation in medical devices leads to improved levels of clinical outcome. Medical devices increasingly shoulder some of the challenges in diagnosis and surgical treatment. There are things that computers can do in analysis of images or programming of surgical lasers that surpass human ability. In theory, this should allow you to spend more time and energy on the patient and their experience. But even here it can prove tempting to replace face-to-face interaction with a computer screen. EHR is a good example of technology failing the overall experience. Patients say their doctor now pays more attention to a computer screen than to them, while doctors often say EHR slows them down. That's a lose-lose situation. As you consider adopting any given technology in your practice, ask yourself if the technology will likely have a positive or negative effect

145

on the customer's overall experience. Technology should only be added if it serves to enhance the customer experience. If it is intended to replace a function currently performed by staff, then you need to make sure that it allows your team to focus on higher-level interaction and engagement with patients.

One part of the medical appointment experience longing for improvement is the stack of forms waiting when a patient arrives. At some point, this became a justification for time spent in the waiting room. But like the recommendation to eliminate the waiting room, technology is available to digitize form filling, appointment scheduling, reminders, and insurance verification. These functions can move from being an annoyance to a convenience for both your patients and your staff, saving face time for more valuable interaction.

THIRTY-FIVE

When We Fail

In every service business, things don't always go as planned. It's the same in a medical practice, whether a patient arrives late, the doctor's running behind, or a piece of equipment breaks down. Stuff happens that can negatively impact the overall experience. What do you do to handle these daily obstacles? In the hospitality industry, an entire science has emerged around the concept of service recovery. In short, this means enacting protocols and processes that kick in whenever something goes wrong or a customer complains.

Interestingly, the data on customer satisfaction yield a powerful finding: When the business promptly responds to an issue or complaint, customer loyalty goes up! Marriott discovered this in their customer surveys, where those who had complained actually rated the overall experience better when the staff promptly and successfully resolved the issue. Think about what this means to your practice. You have the ability to turn

" WHEN THE BUSINESS PROMPTLY RESPONDS TO AN ISSUE OR COMPLAINT, CUSTOMER LOYALTY GOES UP!"

a negative moment into potential for even greater patient satisfaction and loyalty. As restaurateur Danny Meyer proclaims, "Whenever something goes wrong, we have the ability to write the next chapter in how the story will turn out." You have that same ability, as long as you prepare and have a system in place to handle it.

Don't require a front line team member to obtain approval before offering something they know will make the customer happy. The Ritz Carlton authorizes employees to resolve issues up to $2000 without having to get a manager's approval. Imagine what a similar practice would look like in your clinic, and what that would communicate to your patients and your team in terms of the level of trust you place in them. You want to resolve the issue as quickly and as best as possible. Have a stack of gift cards in small denominations that can be redeemed at a nearby cafe or sandwich shop. Offering these to a disrupted patient can go a long way to soothing tension.

Don't leave your front line employees stranded. Define protocols for service recovery and give your team the authority and discretion to resolve any customer issues. Putting trust in your team to do the right thing does wonders for staff morale and confidence. Then stand back and witness the impact on both the customer and employee experience.

SERVICE RECOVERY PARADOX

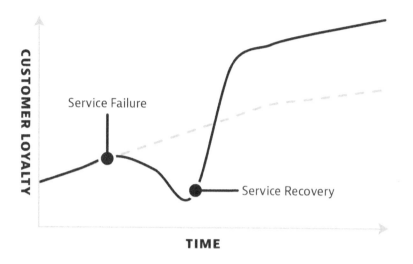

Customer Loyalty / Time

Service Failure

Service Recovery

- - - Customers Without Service Failure

───── Customers With Service Failure & Successful Recovery

THIRTY-SIX

Always Get Better

The Japanese word *kaizen*, which literally translates to "improvement," represents the philosophy that an organization should strive to continuously improve all aspects of its operation. Car buyers in the 1980s benefitted from this approach, as Japanese automobiles earned a reputation for styling and reliability that was unmatched at the time. American car companies have now largely caught up as they also adopted continuous improvement in their manufacturing; quality and reliability across all auto manufacturers is now far greater than a generation ago. It's just a shame that too many dealership salespeople haven't yet improved their selling skills.

For your patient experience, continuous improvement is the mantra you want to adopt. Perfecting is a verb associated with your craft and the reality means that you are never truly finished. The goal is to get better and better over time, which is an ongoing process. Working to improve the level of service and enhance the customer experience becomes part of everybody's day job at the practice. And key to these efforts are the data you collect.

Let's start with complaints, which arise when something goes wrong from the perspective of the customer. This type of data is immediate and may require urgent attention. The problem is that most people don't complain even when they have an issue. Customer surveys consistently find that only one out of every twenty-five patients with a complaint will actually say something; nearly all (96%) keep quiet. Since silence can be deadly when it comes to patient referrals, it's critical to have multiple early warning systems in place so that you get the data you need in order to continuously improve.

Patient surveys are a good source of information, with many options that make this easy to implement: from paper-based or e-mail surveys to more sophisticated software. Inviting immediate feedback gives your team the opportunity to intervene and take corrective action before a negative incident spreads via word-of-mouth or "word-of-mouse."

" NO MATTER HOW GREAT THE FEEDBACK YOU RECEIVE, NEVER DECLARE VICTORY."

Third-party mystery shoppers can provide a detailed view of your practice from people who don't have an established relationship with the practice. Good mystery shoppers will point out items that current patients may forgive or that you never noticed yet can be detrimental to attracting new patients. Their objectivity is difficult to get from employees or well-meaning patients, who may not speak up for fear of offending you.

How you interpret and use the data are important. You want to get to the bottom of any negative experience brought to light by a patient so you can prevent it from happening in the future. But caution is warranted to make sure the data and feedback are used to improve processes rather than indict people. Too many doctors want to place blame for a complaint on a staff member, when often it would be more productive to (1) acknowledge a failure to properly set or manage expectations, (2) offer necessary training and (3) provide regular feedback to hold employees accountable to the desired standard of performance. That is what it means and what it takes to be an effective leader in your practice.

No matter how great the feedback you receive, never declare victory. Always strive to improve how you do what you do. Your patients will appreciate this effort and your practice will thrive because of it. Because the standard of customer care across medical office environments remains low, every action you take to improve will likely have an outsized increase in perceived value in the mind of your customer.

—THIRTY-SEVEN—

Small Is the New Big

One of the most important insights this book has to offer is that the small changes you make often have the greatest impact in terms of overall patient experience. The principle that little changes can have a great impact pertains to all the aspects of a customer-focused practice.

Many doctors get excited when they first start compiling a list of all the changes they want to make and then intimidated when they see how long the list is and start adding up dollar signs. Some of these (e.g., remodeling) are both expensive and time-consuming as well as potentially disruptive to practice flow and revenue. These large changes should take a back-seat to what can be thought of as subtle-yet-significant small changes.

John DiJulius became known as a master of making hundreds of small changes to improve the client experience at his John Roberts Salon and Spa. With multiple locations around

Cleveland, he was able to command $80 when the average cost of a haircut in the city was around $20. "It's a pair of scissors and a straight line," he would say in deference to what he views as his true advantage. He and his staff work tirelessly to eliminate negative cues that frequently exist in hair salons. In doing so, he created such a compelling environment that he achieved his own goal to make price irrelevant through outstanding customer service. He has taken the same principles and helped hundreds of clients in hospitality, dining and even healthcare.

Seek input from your team early and often in the process. You will find that most of the ideas they have for improvement fall into the small category. Your staff are your eyes and ears in the office, as they spend more time in more places with your patients than you do. They are full of ideas but often lack the courage to speak up, believing that their ideas wouldn't be considered. Don't allow your eyes and ears in the office to go blind and deaf.

As you think small, you will discover that many ideas are relatively easy to implement and have little or no cost. As your team sees that their input is taken seriously and acted on, their confidence builds as they personally experience what it means to have an impact on improving the practice. If big changes can be thought of as the Disneyland moments in life, then small changes should be thought of as everyday living.

Start out by thinking small and paying attention to the little changes that should be made. This is where the greatest power lies in terms of influencing perception and enhancing the patient experience.

PROMOTION

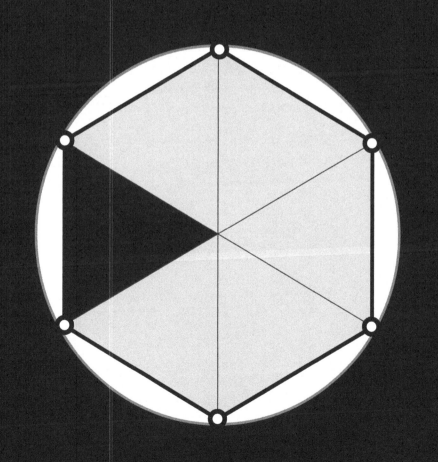

PROMOTION

Practices are polarized when it comes to advertising, either wanting to do a lot of it or absolutely none. The insights here are intended to expand your view of what it means to promote your practice, with a bias towards building your practice with marketing that is affordable, sustainable, and often more effective than a traditional advertising plan and budget.

Shifting resources away from paid advertising towards investing in a foundation of excellent customer service will put your practice in a position to engage patients in a more personal and meaningful way. This paves the way for the ultimate approach to market your practice, which is to allow the patient experience to be the marketing.

—THIRTY-EIGHT—

Meet Your New Competitor

You may believe that the competition for your practice is made up of the other nearby practices in your specialty. In one sense this is correct as patients make a choice between practices for the services they seek.

From a consumer standpoint, however, you have a competitor in your midst that didn't meaningfully exist twenty years ago. It's been brought to the forefront because the ability for anyone to access information at anytime now has been placed in the palm of one's hand via the smartphone.

You are now also competing for the attention of your customer against all modern distractions. If you want to capture the time and money of your customer, you need to command their attention. And if what you are saying or doing isn't engaging or relevant, your potential customer can tune you out by simply pulling out their phone.

This has several implications for the medical practice. First, any effort to promote your practice and its services now has a higher bar in terms of being able to connect with a target audience. Once you do reach them, what happens when people visit your website? Is it sufficiently compelling to make them want to learn more? When they step inside your practice, you want to make sure every step along the patient experience - from arrival to patient history, from diagnostic workup to clinical evaluation and then from consultation to next steps - is sufficiently engaging so that you maintain attention.

Failure to pay attention to the patient's attention can be seen in several ways. They don't call to book an appointment. They fail to show up. They listen politely and nod their head but have already checked out mentally. All of these mean "no" when it comes to patients taking advantage of what you offer.

In our over-stimulated and time-starved world, you are fundamentally competing for the attention of the consumer when trying to attract them to your practice. Understanding this principle will help you focus more energy on what can be done to be more engaging and compelling with your patients. The better you become at keeping their attention, the easier it will be attracting it in the first place.

THIRTY-NINE

The Best Advertising

If you were to ask for the best method for advertising your practice, the answer is the type you don't have to pay for. The more you move along the continuum towards outstanding service and memorable experiences, the less you will need to depend on paid advertising as a means of growing the business.

Geek Squad founder Robert Stephens once said, "Advertising is the price you pay for being unremarkable." When he first started Geek Squad (which has since been acquired by Best Buy), he had no money for advertising. This forced him to get creative when promoting his in-home computer repair service and led him to believe that every customer interaction was a form of advertising.

Advertising is not good or bad. It just tends to be misunderstood and misused as a means of promoting the practice.

The purpose of advertising should be limited to a singular objective: create greater awareness of your practice and what it offers. That is all. Advertising will not convince someone to have a procedure. That involves education and consultation, both of which happen at the practice and not in an ad. Medical procedures are often a highly considered purchase decision, meaning it weighs on the consumer emotionally as well as financially.

Most medical practice advertising tries to do too much, often invoking a specific call-to-action: "Call now!"; "Take advantage of our special!"; "Limited time offer!" The services you offer as a medical professional are not traditional retail offerings that might benefit from creating a sense of urgency for the consumer. What you do as a doctor is more valuable and more lasting than what can be purchased in a store.

" ADVERTISING IS NOT GOOD OR BAD. IT JUST TENDS TO BE MISUNDERSTOOD AND MISUSED"

Should you choose to invest in paid advertising, be careful not to damage the brand reputation that you have worked hard to establish. Take a step back and ask this question — if you're so good, why do you need to advertise in the first place? Many a consumer thinks this way when it comes to healthcare. When your advertising includes some mention of price or discount, it signals to the consumer that the decision should be based on price rather than on value received. That is the essence of commoditization and it reduces value both financially and from a brand reputation perspective.

By its very nature, advertising is interruptive and seeking our attention with limited time — not the best conditions in which to convince a person who to trust regarding highly personal and emotional healthcare decisions. Consumers aren't stupid and have largely tuned out the bombardment of advertising messages. It's far better to have an engaging experience that warrants our attention.

If you do advertise, it should be one of the last things you do after you have exhausted all other (typically far less expensive) means of marketing your practice. As far as your budget is concerned, the best kind of advertising is often no advertising; or rather, a practice so strong that it speaks for itself.

—FORTY—

Know Your Audience

Those of you who are hell bent on advertising need to think seriously about what gets put in that page of the newspaper, local magazine or on the radio. Many print ads seem to have been written by the doctors themselves; they often include a headshot or photo, sometimes standing proudly next to some medical device, a description of where they were trained, and some copy about being the first, the best, or the only doctor who can do what they do. The same thinking seems to permeate radio and TV spots, where many of the precious seconds are devoted to talking about the doctor and their qualifications rather than the solution to the consumer's problem. This approach is just not going to work to attract a significant number of people to pick up the phone and call your office. This is because what you care about as a doctor is not what your audience typically cares about as a consumer.

" WHAT YOU CARE ABOUT AS A DOCTOR IS NOT WHAT YOUR AUDIENCE TYPICALLY CARES ABOUT AS A CONSUMER. "

Writing good advertising copy is a skill best left to a professional or at least someone besides yourself. As a doctor, you are far too close to what you do to be effective at writing for the audience you are trying to attract. It's too hard for you to be objective and convey a message that will appeal to your audience yet may have little or no personal meaning to you. This holds true across all mediums - print, radio, TV, outdoor (billboard) and digital.

The truth is that you are not your customer. Recognizing this will help you delegate the advertising design to others who understand how to properly construct the key message. Failure to recognize this will create a nice looking ad that soothes your ego but doesn't get people to visit your website or call your practice.

FORTY-ONE

Your Website Matters

It is astounding how many doctors do not have their own website, seemingly content to be listed in an online directory or on industry websites, such as Healthgrades, with patient reviews. The majority of your patients are spending time online to learn, to shop, to play, and to work. When exploring options in healthcare, the internet is the first place they go before talking to anybody else. According to a study conducted by Software Advice, the percentage of patients who have consulted online review sites has jumped from 82 to 94% just in the past year. The internet has become the new standard for learning about a practice.

A generation ago, most doctors paid for a listing in the Yellow Pages, and some paid extra in order to get more space on the page. This was how people found out about your practice. When was the last time you looked something up in the Yellow Pages? The ways that consumers find you have changed significantly in the past ten to twenty years. Having your own practice website provides much more opportunity than could ever be realized in a static space contained in a thick book.

As you design your website (or redesign it, if it's been awhile), a whole new world opens up where topics and questions that were generated during an office visit may be handled outside of the visit, often before they ever come to your practice. Patient education, forms, scheduling, payments and access to medical records are all items that can and should be integrated on your website, freeing up precious time to enhance the overall experience when patients are physically in your office.

A well-designed website allows you to showcase much more than could ever be done during a visit. You can post profiles of doctors and staff members, blog about hot topics that will be of interest to your patients, incorporate online scheduling, and display reviews by your patients. A website allows you to highlight your involvement in your community and describe what types of patients might be most attracted to your style and philosophy of practice.

Websites are not expensive to build or manage, but require an investment of time, which is why many website companies exist. For a single monthly fee, the best ones provide design, content refreshment, upgrades, search engine optimization, and aggregation of all your patient reviews without absorbing your or your staff's time.

Your website is an essential component of your practice and extends your impact by eliminating restrictions of time (it's available 24/7) and space (you don't need a larger footprint). It can make a strong first impression and serve as a highly effective tool to promote your practice, educate the community, and serve many needs of your patients.

Your website is likely the first stage in the customer experience for your patients. Thus, it also serves as the first step in the doctor-patient relationship, one that you can no longer afford to ignore. If you aren't on the web, how do you expect patients to know you exist or find you?

Reviews
Not Referrals

Handing out your business card to patients and asking them to refer others used to be acceptable. Now it comes across as desperate, as if you have no other means of obtaining new patients. It can also come across as a hard-sell tactic.

There are far better ways to stimulate referrals. But first, a bit more on the business card. Some marketing professionals say they are obsolete, especially with smartphones and the ability to airdrop or similarly share contact information. Business cards may be old school, but they still work. It's just that their function has changed. When handing over your business card, it should be paired with the question, "What else can we do for you?" This simple inquiry conveys far more than the question, as it empowers the patient to know they can reach out to you in the future and is nice as a means of extending the experience and your relationship. Doctors who include their cell phone number tell me that very few people actually call and that the fear of being abused is not realized. This simple addition on your business card communicates "We're here for you" in a way that is personal and powerful.

Because patients have come to expect doctors to ask for referrals, you want to replace this with something far more valuable – a review. Having a patient take the time to write a review gives them an opportunity to brag about you and your staff so that you don't have to. It's the type of third-party endorsement that, collectively, is more credible than an advertisement or a featured testimonial of some big celebrity. The operative word here being "collectively." A large number of patient reviews is an automatic signal of quality in the mind of the consumer.

Do not fear the occasional negative review. Rather, embrace it as a means of getting feedback that your practice can use to improve. Over time, and as long as most of your patients are satisfied and submitting positive reviews, the negative ones will not have much long-term impact. But if you only have a handful of reviews because you don't actively cultivate them, you risk being perceived as a poor provider of medical care. If one or more of that small sample of opinions is negative, your rating will be low. A low rating means consumers will pass you by as they seek out a doctor for their needs. This is why having a strategy and system in place to get patients to review you should be lockstep with having a solid website.

Never Ask for a Referral. Always ask for a review.

—FORTY-THREE—

Internal Beats External

When it comes to growing revenue, most businesses understand that it is easier to do more business with a current customer than to cultivate a new one. Customer acquisition can be very expensive, as any doctor who advertises or does other paid promotions can attest. This business reality has led to a distinction within the medical practice between internal marketing and external marketing. Broadly speaking, internal marketing costs little to employ and involves activities within your practice aimed at your current patients, while external marketing involves paying to broadcast your message beyond your practice.

The big mistake most practices make is believing they already do sufficient internal marketing and have exhausted its possibilities, forcing them to look externally to attract more patients and more business. In some ways, external marketing is "sexier" and more appealing because it involves spending money, hiring an agency, interacting with local media outlets, and seeing your name in lights. That's an expensive ego trip.

Internal marketing is as much a philosophy as it is a set of tactics. The entire practice can get creative how to promote within as well as beyond the physical office, just as Geek Squad did with computer repair as noted in an earlier insight. "When you have no money to advertise, everything you do becomes a means to promote your business," said founder Robert Stephens.

When patients come to your practice, leverage that time to make them aware of new services you offer and don't assume they already know about the full range of services you have available. This can be done visually (posters, signage, in-office videos), interactively (adding a simple question to the intake form, "Would you like to learn more about_____?"), and proactively by having staff members ask questions when it appears that a patient might benefit from one of your services.

Be careful to avoid having every bit of wall or counter space filled with messaging about your services. It comes across as cluttered and can seem overly promotional as a nonstop series of advertising billboards in your office. Having a rack of brochures or haphazardly placed brochure holders amounts to a "self service" approach to education. This is lazy, impersonal and ineffective. Instead, keep the brochures within reach so that you or a staff member can personally offer a specific brochure to the patient and encourage them to read it and learn more about a procedure you are recommending.

Staging events for patients, ranging from procedure/condition specific webinars to open houses to community outings are great ways to stay connected with your patient base and expand your reach to their network of family, friends and co-workers. This leverages internal marketing in a way that reaches beyond your patient base without additional spending. When hosting events, expand the invitation list to include other referral sources. This can be other practices as well as nearby businesses (so they can learn more about what you do). All of this builds your presence with patients and your community.

Communicate services and events to your patients through multiple mediums - website, direct mail, postcards, email and text. Your practice management database and add-on software applications from marketing vendors can efficiently help engage current patients to do more business with your practice.

Make every member of your team part of the internal marketing program. If someone on your staff has had a specific treatment or procedure you offer, allow them to be your ambassador and answer questions from interested patients. If the doctor had the procedure, by all means tell patients. Knowing that their doctor takes their own medicine adds huge credibility.

Go internal first. Only go external when you believe you've truly exhausted all possible promotion strategies within your current patient population.

FORTY-FOUR

The Alumni Network

Patients you've performed surgery on are the alumni network for your practice and remain a great untapped resource for practice growth. Doctors already understand that current patients are their primary source of new ones. However, research and consulting by my firm over the years suggests that most practices lack the systems or protocols to consistently track patient referral behavior.

What typically happens when an existing patient refers a new one is... nothing. If doctors can acknowledge the power of patients to generate new clients, why are there no systems in place to further encourage this process?

Some practices believe that happy patients will tell their friends and no further action needs to be taken. Once upon a time, that may have been true. But our world is far different, especially when it comes to how people interact with those who provide services.

In an earlier insight, we discussed how the best advertising comes free of charge as your customer experience does most of the work in generating new business. Outreach and a positive way to encourage referrals must be part of that experience.

You would be wise to take a strategic approach in viewing your current patients as potential ambassadors for your practice. It is far more critical to recognize their efforts than to provide a reward; incentive programs are nice but generally appeal to a small subset of patients who look to be rewarded for everything they do. They are the ones who say, "I can bring you a bunch of patients, but what will you do for me?" and rarely deliver. Regulations prevent paying directly for referrals from any sources, so any gifts you provide should be cleared by your legal counsel (typically those that are small in monetary value pass the test).

The standard should be that when someone refers a patient, you have a system in place to thank them and then to keep track of the source of all new patients who were referred by existing ones. Thanking your referring patients in writing or in person are ways of making them feel valued for the effort they made. Sending a handwritten note is likely to be even more appreciated.

This type of acknowledgement is priceless in the mind of the patient and reinforces their status as an alumni of your practice. You may also want to adopt a communications calendar that includes practice updates, milestones and events. Each time you communicate with your patient base, make sure that what you are sending adds value to your existing relationship (based on the principle that you want to give before you get anything in return). Keeping your patients updated on new trends in your specialty that affect their health is a good example of adding value.

Events that are planned specifically for your alumni are musts as part of an ongoing relationship with patients you've already treated. This is why you get invited to your high school or college reunion - it serves as a way to reconnect and add to the original experience. Events require an investment of time and resources that may not pay off immediately, which is fine. The investment you are making is in the long-term relationship with this group.

Events can take place inside your practice or out in the community. Thinking about your practice as a gathering spot for activities is a way to meaningfully engage with patients outside of a medical exam. You accomplish the same when you decide to buy a few hundred tickets to a local sporting event and invite your patients to come as your guests. Even those that don't participate will notice the invitation and appreciate the effort being made; doing these things keeps you "top of mind" in their world and readies their answer when someone asks them who to see for the types of services you are offering.

These tactics are part of extending the patient experience - the fifth stage as described in the earlier insight that highlighted the 5E Model. Your current patients are the best source for new patients, especially if your practice is customer-focused. The key is having systems in place to make it easy for patients to make referrals, easy for you to acknowledge their effort, and easy for the community to stay engaged with your practice.

Beyond Bedside Manner

FORTY-FIVE

Everything Communicates

Many doctors think that communication applies to how people verbally interact with one another. That's only part of the equation.

When it comes to marketing your practice, everything communicates. Everything. You need to pay attention to things that you previously didn't regard as part of your brand, because everything that happens in your practice is part of your brand, much more so than the advertising or other forms of promotion that you may be doing.

"Everything" can be divided into two broad categories: what patients see and what patients hear.

Patients don't just see your advertising; they also see forms, signs, employee badges...each of these is part of the brand identity. Even the titles you give to employees matter and warrant special consideration as they can boost self-esteem as well as your brand.

You are well advised to take a walking tour through your practice; you may be shocked by how much stuff is laying around. Most practices have a clutter problem, from worn out pieces of paper hastily taped to a wall that communicate payment policies to generic brochures intended to educate but not serving their intended purpose very well. These visual cues make as much of an impression as furniture and art on your walls, and you want to make sure that everything patients see is consistent with the brand you want to create for your practice.

Patients hear your words and more. Words matter when you and your team are speaking. Keep explanations simple in how you and your staff members describe each and every aspect of patient care. One good test is whether or not a sixth grader can understand what's being said. If not, the explanation needs to be further simplified.

Similarly, spending time to train staff and make sure everyone knows their script keeps everybody on the same page and adds to that brand consistency. When a staff member tells a patient, "I don't know," it should always be followed by, "and I know who does. Let me get that answer for you." This communicates that you care enough to make sure the question gets answered.

Non-verbal cues are just as important; in fact, studies show that words by themselves only account for 7% of how we communicate and understand others. The rest is communicated through body language, facial expressions and the way we deliver speech (tone, volume, etc.).

As described earlier, your brand is in many regards the promise of an experience. That promise is fulfilled or broken mainly by what patients see and what they hear when they are in your practice. Because everything communicates something, pay close attention to how each detail impacts the overall patient experience.

Beyond Bedside Manner

PRICE

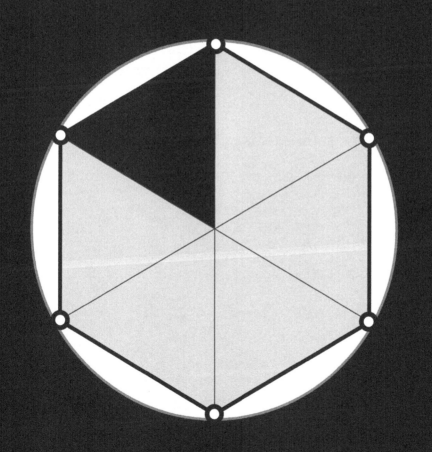

PRICE

The topic of price is saved for last because that is where it belongs as patients are learning about procedures and whether they are appropriate.

Price is well understood by consumers yet greatly misunderstood by doctors. By sharpening your understanding of buying psychology, you and your team can take control and discuss price in its proper context as part of the overall decision-making process.

This section of insights is intended to help you resist the temptation to devalue your services when your fees are challenged. Don't allow price to be the Achilles' heel in your practice. Make price less relevant by providing outstanding service as part of a great experience so that patients want to spend their money on what you offer.

FORTY-SIX

Is It Really About Price?

When talking about your services and how much you charge, it's helpful to remember this: *It's not about price unless you make it about price.*

Early in the decision process, most people lack the proper context to understand and appreciate cost relative to value. Many practices handle the discussion of price poorly because they lack a strategic framework surrounding cost, benefits and value. Instead of leading with benefits, they focus on cost. Counselors either bring up price too early in the decision process or reflexively answer when the patient's first question is "How much is it?" This scenario is reinforced every time a patient is exposed to consumer advertising of elective procedures with messages that focus on how much something costs rather than the value and benefits that are achieved.

Instead of taking the bait and allowing price to become the focus, counselors should pause and ask a simple question: "Why is price the first question on your mind?" There are more important questions in the patient's mind that need to be resolved before they get into discussion of price. Once you've helped them understand the benefits, risks, and how you and your practice will care for them, you have hopefully built up sufficient value and trust so that the discussion of price can now take place. It's no longer the "hot button" because you chose not to make it one; rather, you chose to address the most important questions first to assess candidacy and address overall expectations.

What doctors and all staff in the practice need to understand is that price is typically fourth or fifth on the list of factors provided by people who have made a decision. In LASIK, for example, patients routinely rank price behind (1) assessing will it work for me? (2) recommendation from a friend, (3) referral from another doctor, and (4) confidence in the surgeon.

Cost is often cited as the key reason for why people choose not to go forward with an elective procedure. What's often going on is that there hasn't been sufficient value created in the mind of the consumer to go forward. In other words, the practice doesn't recognize that it's about failure to demonstrate value and not the price itself. People make choices everyday about how to spend their hard-earned money. Relative to other uses of their discretionary income, this option doesn't become a priority.

Some doctors wrongly believe that by lowering their prices they will grow their business. All they are really doing is under-valuing their services by making price the focus of the decision.

There are many ways to talk about fees and costs that patients have to bear directly. Because you are dealing with individuals and their health, you should frame the discussion as an investment in self. Just look at the change in patient comments from before to after the procedure. In LASIK, the typical comment beforehand – "It seems expensive" – shifts to "I wish I had done it sooner" afterwards. From that point forward, they appreciate the value and realize the investment they are making in their own well-being.

It's critical to understand how consumers view price in the context of the overall decision-making process. Consumers will want to buy your services based on trust and confidence, not price. Nobody really wants cheap surgery; what they want is a great outcome and a great experience throughout the process. Help them achieve that and everybody wins - your patient and your practice.

—FORTY-SEVEN—

"Why is it so expensive?"

When a consumer asks the question, "Why is it so expensive?," it's a clear indication that they lack context and a frame of reference to understand and appreciate the value proposition of your offering. This is a normal question people ask, especially early on in their decision-making process. In *Selling the Invisible,* author Harry Beckwith sheds light on how much people should charge for their services. In what he terms the Resistance Principle, if 20% of your customers are not complaining about your price, then your prices are set too low. Within this group, about half will complain about price no matter what. The other half are made up of patients who want a deal, arrived with a price in mind, or had already established a budget amount to spend. That's okay. As Beckwith says, a little resistance is good.

We are conditioned to make decisions based on price, and when there is no apparent discount, consumers reflexively ask, "Why is it so expensive?" without really ever thinking through the question. To you and your staff, this often comes across as offensive or insulting, as if questioning your fee schedule is an attack on your medical expertise. Or you assume they are looking for the cheapest provider.

In reality, many people are doing their due diligence and need reassurance to resolve their own conflicts about spending money. Consumers have been trained over the years by retailers to make decisions based on price rather than on other more important criteria. Price shopping is reinforced by sales events (Black Friday, Cyber Monday), coupons, buy-one-get-one offers...you name it.

Their line of questioning is simply part of what they've been trained to do, and you can be prepared by having a scripted response that is first and foremost non-defensive in tone. Your role is to help resolve the conflict between unwillingness to pay and desire for the best treatment.

" CONSUMERS HAVE BEEN TRAINED OVER THE YEARS BY RETAILERS TO MAKE DECISIONS BASED ON PRICE RATHER THAN ON OTHER MORE IMPORTANT CRITERIA. "

What you say should help the patient understand the value of everything you and your team bring to the table, which can include technology, outcomes, convenient hours, and, perhaps most important, a caring and empathetic approach that puts the patient first.

People understand that it costs money to perform your services on their behalf. You want to make sure you have people on your team who can answer questions about price and communicate in a way that builds trust and confidence. These staff members, who must be comfortable talking about money matters, also need to have strong listening skills to understand the patient's concerns. From there, responding in a way that best fits each patient's situation is paramount. There is no "one size fits all" response. Planning and role-playing are requirements to fully develop communication skills around discussions of price. Examples of responses include relating your fees to other similar-costing items, showing the fee as a cost-per-day comparable to other daily purchases, and positioning the expenditure as an investment in self.

Recall when you last went shopping for a one-time purchase in unfamiliar territory. You probably wondered why it cost so much. Your patients are no different when it comes to paying directly for procedures.

FORTY-EIGHT

Talking About Money

Money influences how we live our daily lives; you would think it would be an easy topic to discuss. Just search the term "money management" online and you will find there are over five thousand books devoted to the subject.

Money is a tricky topic. Consumer research maintains that any given consumer can hold opposing philosophies about money (e.g., both desiring it and condemning it). This is evident among people who believe you get what you pay for, while at the same time bargain hunting to get more than they pay for.

In healthcare, discussion of money used to be off the table. Somebody else was footing the bill, so patients said yes to doctor's recommendations without too much concern for cost. Doctors didn't need to be good at talking about money and could focus their energy on clinical care.

Regardless of specialty, patients are now being asked to foot more or all of the bill. As consumers, they are seeking to better understand what they are getting for their money. Many doctors seem to struggle with this financial aspect of the relationship, as "moneytalk" may conflict with their intended role as a healer. Just the same, many doctors see themselves as above money matters, exclaiming, "I didn't go to business school. I went to medical school."

Too late. Forces have changed this dynamic in the doctor-patient relationship. Skyrocketing costs for health insurance (premiums, deductibles and scope of coverage) have forced consumers to understand the relationship between the value of a certain procedure and what it costs. The lack of access or perceived quality in traditional insurance coverage for primary care has led to the rise of concierge models, where doctors and patients transact directly and eliminate the middleman and much of the bureaucracy. And an explosion of technology that addresses a wide range of lifestyle-enhancing elective procedures brings discretionary spending to the forefront in medical care.

Consider these forces alongside the immediate availability of information online. It should become clear that your practice needs to be fluent in talking about money including fees, the value you give for the price you charge, financing options, and objection-handling. It's fine if you don't want to have that conversation. Hire and train people on your team to handle these discussions; people with sales backgrounds often have learned how to talk about money with ease. Contrary to what you might think, patients are actually more impressed when the practice has a good command of the money matters that affect their decision-making.

It's time for you to accept that money is as much a part of medicine as the clinical care you strive to provide. Your patients are already there. Are you?

FORTY-NINE

Don't Compete on Price

Healthcare is an inherently personal transaction between a patient and a doctor. While it's true that consumers are increasingly seeking value for their dollar, this does not mean that practices should act like Walmart or online retail and compete on price. Sadly, few doctors understand how lowering price can devastate the financials of their practice. Those who go down this path often fall prey to mistakenly associating an increased demand for services with pricing that is a little bit lower than the next practice. The thinking continues that once patients see that the offering is a better deal with the same service at a lower price, they will come in droves and the practice will make it up in volume.

But the financial norms of medical practices are different than other businesses like Walmart, whose expertise in supply chain management and vendor negotiation enables them to roll back prices as part of their value proposition. With fixed overhead typically 50-70% of collected revenue, as well as often high variable costs associated with each procedure, it's challenging to increase bottom line profitability when you decrease average revenue from each encounter or procedure.

" TRYING TO COMPETE BY LOWERING PRICES IS A RACE TO THE BOTTOM AND DEATH SPIRAL FOR THE MEDICAL PRACTICE."

Practices can see a temporary increase in response to lowering price. Demand goes up, overall revenue may increase and (if you are very lucky), some additional profit may be generated. But there are opportunity costs that often get left out of the calculation. Everybody is working harder rather than smarter, leading to exhaustion and burnout. Practice reputation takes a hit as consumers learn to wait for the next "sale" when the price will once again be lower. The medical practice gets lumped together with the clothing store that has an end-of-season sale because it needs to move inventory and make room for the new fashion. Medical practices don't have inventory that needs to be moved in order to free up working capital. The financial circumstance is wholly different, and this gets lost on the consumer, whose instinct to make a price-based decision only gets reinforced.

Over time, you will find that your margins – gross, operating and net – all suffer as you work harder just to keep up with what you likely would have earned had you sustained lower procedure volumes at higher prices.

A low price strategy is not sustainable. Trying to compete by lowering prices is a race to the bottom and a death spiral for the medical practice.

FIFTY

Price Influences Perception

As consumers, we maintain an association between price and quality that lies deep within our minds. The bond is instinctive to the point that when we see something that seems cheaper than what we expect, the quality automatically comes into question. In short, we are hardwired to believe that the more expensive something is, the better it is. While this may not always prove to be true, research in multiple studies shows the difficulty consumers face in separating these two variables.

One of the best studies on price comes from wine tasting. Researchers at Stanford and CalTech collaborated to do a more formal version of the "brown bag" approach, where people try to guess which wines taste better before knowing the price of the bottle. These informal studies often surprise people because cheaper wines are commonly preferred over more expensive ones. In the formal research, subjects were asked to taste a pair of wines and told ahead of time the price, one costing $10 per bottle and the other $90. Not surprisingly, people preferred the more expensive one. They did it again with a different pair of wines, one at $5 and the other at $45. Again, the same outcome of preference favored the more expensive offering.

In each pair tasted, the wine was identical. In the first pair, the more expensive $90 wine was poured in each glass. In the second pair, the cheaper $5 wine was poured into both glasses. This result demonstrates the power that price has in influencing our perception of quality, especially when there are no other cues available.

What made this study more unique is that participants also had brain responses measured via functional MRI. In the seconds immediately following each sip, stimulation was greater in the area of the brain that registers pleasurable experiences. Indeed the medial Orbito-Frontal Cortex, (mOFC) showed significantly greater response when tasting the wine labeled as more expensive. When price labels were removed, participants consistently rated the least expensive wine as their favorite (just as in the brown bag studies). These findings further reinforce the power of pricing to influence perception, even beyond what some may call "snob appeal."

Price can also impact perception after the fact, as illustrated in one study involving healthy consumers and a new fast-acting pain reliever. One group was told the new drug costs

" REMEMBER THAT THE PRICE YOU CHARGE INFLUENCES THE PERCEPTION PATIENTS HAVE ABOUT YOUR QUALITY. "

$2.50 per pill, while the other was told it had been marked down to 10 cents a pill. Participants in both groups were given light electrical shocks on the wrist to determine pain tolerance both before and after taking the pill. 85% of the full-price pill group reported less pain afterwards compared to 61% of the discount-price pill group. Considering that a sugar pill was given to both groups, the power of price perception helps explain the difference.

This type of research should help you understand how your patients view the fee schedule for your offerings. In some instances, they are going to go price shopping to see what other doctors charge for the procedure. In other cases, they may be comparing your fees to an internal reference point they have around price and what they think something should cost. Price is a surrogate for quality, especially when it's difficult to objectively judge quality. Always remember that the price you charge influences the perception patients have about your quality.

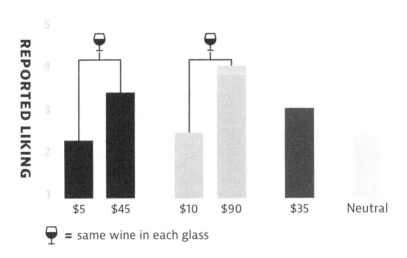

INFLUENCE OF PRICE ON WINE TASTING PREFERENCE

= same wine in each glass

FIFTY-ONE

Do Not Discount

Any time you discount your services, especially early on in the patient discovery/decision process, you are undercutting this long-held consumer association between price and quality. Specifically, discounting signals that your offering may not be high quality. Discounting also signals that you are neither comfortable nor confident with your fee schedule.

You may believe that you need to offer a discount in order to close the sale.

Nonsense.

When you discount, you are feeding into the notion that what you offer is the same as what others offer. Your expertise gets commoditized, meaning that it's valued no differently from what other doctors offer. If this were true, then the patient's decision should be based on price, simply because – all else being equal – consumers want to pay less, not more, when making purchase decisions. Every time you discount, you communicate that your services are not special and you are not unique.

This doesn't mean that you shouldn't add value in some other way. When you buy a custom-tailored suit and the store gives you a matching tie, it's a nice gesture that communicates "We understand your need for a good deal" and doesn't have the devastating effect of discounting. For refractive surgeons, it may be a great pair of sunglasses; for the plastic surgeon, a supply of high-end skincare products.

I recall speaking at a client's user meeting for their physician customers; the event was held at the Montage Hotel in Laguna Beach, a high-end property with service to match. The hotel manager joined me on stage for a brief interview about the staff culture and how they strive to exceed guests' expectations. "Do you discount room rates?" I asked. Without hesitation, the manager replied, "Not at all. That would violate our brand." That's precisely what this insight is about.

Resist the temptation to discount. It's unnecessary, and the same "good deal" feeling can be created when you focus on ways to build more value into your offering that will be appreciated by your patient.

FIFTY-TWO

Price Is Not a Lever

Economists use equations to measure the relationship between price and demand. Basically, when a lowering of price leads to a significant increase in demand, the good or service is said to show elastic demand. And when a change in price does not lead to an increase in demand, it is said to have inelastic demand. Certain food items seem to sell better when the price is lower; grocery stores understand this very well, which is why you see LaCroix (or whatever bubbly water you like) fly off the shelves when they lower the price. Gasoline, on the other hand, doesn't see much change in demand as the price per gallon goes up. We still need to drive to get to work.

Healthcare, especially for elective services, does not exhibit elastic demand. In 2001, when the average fee for LASIK was reduced by 25%, demand for the procedure actually fell by about the same rate. Lowering prices did not result in greater demand. This continued for several years until additional technology for the procedure required doctors to raise their fees. Guess what? Demand started rising to approach previous procedure volumes nationally. During that same time period, fees charged by plastic surgeons for breast augmentation steadily increased about 30% and demand more than doubled. When hearing devices are fitted and sold by audiologists, multiple studies have shown that lowering of prices for hearing aids did not result in a corresponding increase in demand.

Each of these examples exhibits characteristics of inelastic demand and demonstrates that people treat their healthcare expenditures differently than most other goods and services. The reasons for this are many, but when lifestyle can be enhanced by a procedure or device, there is a value proposition that is difficult to measure in purely financial terms. Whether the rationale is "improved lifestyle" or "enhanced quality of life," purchase behavior of elective procedures and products tends to behave more similarly to luxury goods and big ticket items, where higher prices are correlated with greater demand.

When setting your fee schedule, remember that price is just one element of the decision process. You want to avoid adjusting (i.e., lowering) prices with the belief that it will lead to increased demand, as healthcare services don't exhibit changes in demand the way that many consumer goods and services do. Further, do not treat price as a lever you can pull to increase demand for your services. It may work temporarily, but as described earlier, the long-term effects can be devastating.

FIFTY-THREE

"How can I afford it?"

For most people, the most expensive purchases they will make in their lifetime are cars and houses. If the only payment option was by cash or check, far fewer people would own cars or homes. These two industries - automotive and housing- together comprise nearly one-fifth of our economy. Without an array of home mortgages, auto loans and auto leasing, the overall economy would be far smaller.

Over the past twenty-five years, financing has made its way into healthcare as a payment option. For practices with elective services, patient financing typically comprises 10% to 30% of practice revenue. Even though it's a fraction of the $3.6 trillion spent overall in healthcare, $171 billion was spent on elective services for thirty-one million consumers in 2018.

While this may seem impressive, recent research suggests that the market for elective procedures could be much larger. While

31 million people said yes, another 34 million people considered but decided to forego these services. Of those who decided against, 72% of them - twenty-five million people - stated they could not afford the services.

" WHAT SMART RETAILERS HAVE KNOWN FOR A LONG TIME: AFFORDABILITY - NOT PRICE - IS THE KEY TO EXPANDING DEMAND. "

These 25 million consumers cannot pay in full at the time of service, no different conceptually from those who can't pay cash for a house or a car. The study, conducted in 2019 by PYMTS, concludes that the market would be 40% larger if patient financing were offered properly and consistently. "These practices are leaving $86.5 billion on the table by not addressing this issue, and these funds would not only benefit their businesses but also boost the wider economy."

The study confirms what smart retailers have known for a long time: Affordability - not price - is the key to expanding demand. The monthly payment has become widely accepted as a means of discretionary spending by consumers. Home entertainment (e.g., Netflix), clothing (e.g., StitchFix) and gym memberships are budgeted alongside utilities, rent/ mortgage and car payments. Financing is a way to make your services affordable via monthly payments. Over time, a well-run patient finance program will enhance your practice; it's been shown to have a positive impact on the patient's impression of the practice when dealt with up front instead of as an afterthought.

But even among those who offer patient financing, most view this as a necessary evil rather than a key tool to build the business. Part of this is because the dominant provider acts like a big bank; patients have been subject to predatory offers (e.g., no interest if paid in full) and fees paid by the doctors simply to offer financing can be far beyond the fees to accept credit cards. Recent innovation and tighter regulation give practices and their patients a safer, better approach resulting in a frictionless financial transaction.

Patient financing is far preferable to discounting your fees. It should be viewed similarly to luxury auto financing, where leasing options greatly expanded demand for more expensive automobiles. Manufacturers focus attention on the monthly payment, not the total price. You should do the same. It will similarly expand demand for your services.

FIFTY-FOUR

The Line of Memorability

When establishing your fee schedule, it's helpful to understand what economists call The Line of Tangibility, which is meant to distinguish goods (which can be touched) from services (which are performed). When it comes to economic value, the more tangible an offering, the easier it is to compare it to similar offerings based on price. Most physical goods are subject to this rule. Once you've chosen the exact model of the exact item you're looking for, chances are good that you will then look to see who offers it at the best price. Amazon makes price comparison exceptionally easy for most small ticket items; other specialty websites such as TrueCar (for automobiles) offer the same on big ticket purchases. If you are selling physical goods, it's become a real challenge to compete on something besides price. This is the essence of commoditization, where there are no differentiating characteristics; one offering is easily substituted by another and price is the only way to determine value.

Services have also become increasingly tangible and commoditized. Automation has made this happen even faster. For example, you probably don't care which ATM you use to get cash unless you have to pay a withdrawal fee. Consumers routinely shop to get the best deal on what they view as equivalent service offerings. This is why you want to recognize which aspects of your offering are either more tangible (and easily comparable) or have value that is assumed. The more tangible your offering, the less able you are to command a premium for your services.

A similar line —The Line of Memorability— exists between services and experiences. Simply put, the more memorable an experience, the greater value ascribed to it by the consumer.

By focusing on doing what is memorable rather than what is tangible, you will improve your customer experience and achieve greater value in the minds and hearts of your customers. Because that is not easily compared, your patients realize that they cannot get what you are offering anyplace else. The more they realize this, the less price becomes an issue.

And unlike price, technology or even clinical skill – each of which can be replicated by somebody else – the customer experience you offer patients becomes part of the DNA of your practice. It cannot be easily duplicated or cloned by another practice down the street.

FIFTY-FIVE

Customer Service Tax

Doctors want to be fairly compensated for services performed. While you want patients to choose you because they believe you are the best at what you do, part of the reason they choose your practice has little to do with your clinical and surgical skill and everything to do with how they are treated as a customer.

Traditional reimbursed healthcare is challenging because you aren't directly rewarded or compensated for providing excellent customer service. Nevertheless, you should focus on this as if you did. One way to do this is to think of your fee schedule as having separate components for clinical care and customer care. This is not dissimilar from being reimbursed separately for professional and facility fees.

Author and consultant John DiJulius goes so far as to advocate for listing customer service as a component of your invoice. He views this as a "customer service tax," making the point that every organization needs to become accountable for providing excellent customer service. The intent is to help you justify the value for what you charge and prevent you from raising fees without providing sufficient value through excellent service as well as clinical outcomes.

" HOW MUCH OF YOUR FEE CAN BE ATTRIBUTED TO THE LEVEL OF CUSTOMER SERVICE YOU PROVIDE?"

For the most part, we dislike paying taxes. But what we dislike even more is when we pay for something and don't receive it. This applies to the level of service you provide in your practice. How much of your fee can be attributed to the level of customer service you provide?

The more value you can create on the customer experience side, the more you can charge. Even better, the more value you create that is not offered by other practices, the more insulated you will be from competitive pressure to lower your fees because there is less to compare.

DiJulius' customer service work with clients across multiple industries shares a common goal: offer such great service that the overall customer experience makes price irrelevant in the minds of your customers.

Having a focus on developing customer protocols is a better way to gain competitive advantage than by focusing on improving your clinical results another percent or two. The real leverage in building a practice is now on the customer side of the equation.

Beyond Bedside Manner

FIFTY-SIX

Fees Must Reflect Value

It's fascinating to observe how doctors determine how much to charge for what they do.

An innovative refractive eye surgeon summarized his frustration about colleagues' resistance to charging sufficient fees for their services. He firmly believed that a doctor's fee schedule is a direct reflection of their self esteem. Doctors may feel an inner conflict between charging patients and their role as healer. Subsequently, a lower fee schedule may be the result of feelings of guilt over having to charge patients directly. While this may not affect every doctor's practice, there is a need for you to find the balance between ego (which could lead you to charge too much) and self esteem (which could mean you charge too little).

As you establish or adjust your fee schedule to include new services, you want to understand that patients will pay for what they value. This is not necessarily the same as what you value. An important distinction here is that while doctors tend to focus on features, patients are focused on benefits. Patients don't value technological innovation nearly as highly as doctors often do.

Sadly, the focus on features shows up routinely in advertising and in how staff members talk with patients considering elective services. Patients expect great technology and don't really care which laser the doctor uses. The root cause of this disconnect is likely the professional meetings, where doctors routinely compare results in an attempt to say "My device is better than the competitor's." While meaningful to doctors and industry, it falls on deaf ears with patients.

What patients do care about is what each of us cares about: "What's in it for me?", also known as WIIFM. When you decide what you are going to charge for the procedure you perform using that technology, you had better understand how to answer the WIIFM for your patients.

 If you are struggling here, re-examine all the benefits of the procedure and all that your practice does to make sure the patient gets to enjoy them. Within that list you will find better ways to describe why you charge what you charge and likely find it more acceptable to your patients.

The WIIFM principle allows for a deeper understanding of their individual goals. This will help you personalize the discussion by focusing on those benefits that align most closely to their goals. Doing so provides a natural bridge between the fees you charge and the value you provide.

FIFTY-SEVEN

You Are What You Charge For

Is Starbucks a coffee shop? The question is neither sarcastic nor rhetorical. When you examine what Starbucks has accomplished over the past thirty years, it's clear they are not just selling coffee.

From an economic viewpoint, the company grew from $2 billion to $26 billion between 1999 and 2019. The number of locations went from 2,500 to over 30,000 worldwide in the same time span. Meanwhile, the price of coffee futures as a commodity fluctuated, yet ended exactly where it started twenty years earlier at a dollar a pound. If someone had asked you twenty years ago to choose to be a coffee manufacturer or a coffee experience provider, the economic results described above make that choice obvious. The value created by Starbucks is a prime example of what the Experience Economy is all about: people willingly seek to save money on commoditized goods and services so they can spend more money and time on experiences. And Starbucks accomplished much of this before they ever spent a dollar on advertising.

Similar to the first question in this book - "What business are you in?" - you should recognize that "You are what you charge for," a principle that helps explain Starbucks' success. They created a coffee drinking experience that introduced new language for the customer to communicate when ordering a cup of coffee, allowing the beverage itself to be fully customized. They created dramatic tension by having customers order at one spot and pick up their beverage at another. They allowed the consumer to fully customize their beverage purchase. They also sell goods ranging from food to branded merchandise, representing about one-fifth of store revenue.

What was once novel - recall the first time you went to a Starbucks - is now mainstream with a sufficiently differentiated offering that compels many of us to pay $5 or more for a cup of coffee. Meanwhile commoditization of coffee still exists. McDonalds charges 99 cents for any size coffee as a way of getting people to their locations. They still make money selling a large coffee for under a dollar. But there's no buzz. You don't hear people talk about the "McDonalds' experience."

The question is, can you create a patient experience to differentiate your medical practice? The answer is yes. The Experience Economy is no longer an idea. It is all around us as customer experience has become the new means of differentiation across many industries.

There is greater economic value to be created by staging and charging for experiences than in providing a service or selling a good. In healthcare, much of what you do for patients is transformational in nature, meaning that the experience is inherently unique to each patient. Your goal is to also make it memorable for each patient as a means of differentiating your services. Given the state of the typical medical practice, the field is wide open for you to innovate in this regard.

You have choices to make that will similarly define what it is you are selling. Eyecare provides an example that can apply to most specialties in determining what you charge for:

Is it for the eyeglasses you sell? (goods)

Is it for the eye examination and testing you perform? (services)

Is it for the unique experience you designed for refractive patients? (experiences)

How you view your business ("What business are you in?") and how you answer the above for your specialty will go a long way in determining what you charge for.

One key caveat is that experience does not substitute for services or goods. Rather, a memorable customer experience is layered on top of outstanding customer service and high quality goods. One theme reinforced through this book is that practices should make sure they are delivering great customer service before attempting to create customer experiences.

The opportunity for you to establish value that is truly appreciated in the mind (and heart) of your customer awaits and will likely be far greater than what you originally conceived. It's all up to you.

PART III:

Deciding to Change

Deciding to Change:
D x V x F > R

The best model of change I've encountered is also among the simplest to explain. It came during a college internship with a management consultant named Kathie Dannemiller. In the 1980s and 90s, Dannemiller Tyson Associates became known globally for their work helping large companies, often with tens of thousands of employees across hundreds of locations, deal with the process of change. Ford, Boeing, US Steel and the United States Postal Service were among the clients they helped in a field known as organizational development. Their expertise as "change agents" helped organizations move from "command and control" to a more participative style of management involving all employees.

Kathie Dannemiller's goal was to help clients not just change but to understand how the change process works and how to foster it within their organizations. Her impact in my life and countless others cannot be overstated; her mentorship influenced my decision to start a consultancy and serve as a change agent for medical device companies and medical practices. Beyond whatever knowledge of marketing or sales I can offer, much of my time has been spent helping clients set and achieve goals for themselves and the organizations they lead on a daily basis.

"Trust the Process" was one of Kathie's more famous sayings, reflecting a deeply held belief that change takes effort as well as time to unfold. A core formula she used with clients (and credited Beckhard and Harris for coming up with it) could be expressed as an equation comprised of four letters:

$$D \times V \times F > R$$

Each of the four letters represents an element required in order for change to take place.

D   **Dissatisfaction**
not being satisfied with the way things currently are

V   **Vision**
a clear picture of what is possible

F   **First Steps**
concrete action items to begin

R   **Resistance to change**
the normal part of how we operate as human beings

When you put this together, you can see that in order for change to occur, you must have dissatisfaction with the current state of affairs, a vision of what the desired state looks like, and defined first steps to get the process started.

As a multiplication formula, if any one of these three components is missing, its product is zero. Because of our innate resistance to change, anything that equals zero will fail to overcome the resistance to change that exists within individuals, groups and organizations. All three elements - dissatisfaction, vision and first steps - must be in place for change to occur.

As you move forward putting to use the insights contained in this book, keep this simple yet powerful formula in mind when deciding how you want to change your practice. While "DVF>R" applies equally to individuals and groups, most of what has been included here starts with you in terms of developing the mindset and then continues with your team of employees in terms of defining what to focus on and then deciding to commit to change.

As described at the beginning of this book, changing your practice to be more customer-focused is as challenging as the clinical expertise you've developed over your career. Doctors who have been on this path of perfecting the patient experience tell me it is rich and rewarding. This is not only good to hear, it makes sense. Succeeding in becoming patient-driven in all aspects of the practice will naturally lead to a better practice culture with greater understanding, respect and appreciation between and among you, your team and your patients. A strong, positive culture becomes the foundation by which you can change and create the type of practice other doctors haven't even dared to dream about.

My challenge is a call to action: Do something. Do it today. When you see something that needs to be changed, identify the D (dissatisfaction). Be willing to put forth your idea of what "better" would look like by stating the V (vision) and propose the initial F (first steps) in the right direction. Be willing to risk what your peers may deem as silly, unnecessary, or even foolhardy. That's the R (resistance) talking, which is what you should expect at first. This is how you build the future. I've never walked into a practice that has a perfect patient experience. It shouldn't be too difficult to find aspects of your practice that you want to change.

It's a journey that never ends, and I trust that you will learn to love it even more as you move closer towards the vision for your practice.

APPENDIX
References and Resources

Books

The Art of People: 11 Simple People Skills That Will Get You Everything You Want by Dave Kerpen. Currency; 2016.

Blue Ocean Strategy: How to Create Uncontested Market Space and Make the Competition Irrelevant by W. Chan Kim and Renée Mauborgne. Harvard Business Review Press; Expanded Edition 2015.

Crossing the Chasm by Geoffrey A Moore. Harper Business; Third edition 2014.

Delivering Happiness: A Path to Profits, Passion, and Purpose by Tony Hsieh. Grand Central; 2013.

Differentiate or Die: Survival in Our Era of Killer Competition by Jack Trout and Steve Rivkin. Wiley; Second edition 2008.

Do The Right Things...Right It Is That Simple; A Step-By-Step Guide To World-Class Performance by Richard Palermo. Strategic Triangle Inc; 2003.

The E-Myth Revisited: Why Most Small Businesses Don't Work and What to Do About It by Michael E. Gerber. Harper Business; Updated edition 2004.

The Essential Drucker: The Best of Sixty Years of Peter Drucker's Essential Writings on Management by Peter Drucker. Harper Business; 2008.

Everything I Know About Business I Learned from the Grateful Dead: The Ten Most Innovative Lessons from a Long, Strange Trip by Barry Barnes PhD and John Perry Barlow. Business Plus; 2012.

The Experience Economy: Work Is Theater & Every Business a Stage by B. Joseph Pine II and James H. Gilmore. Harvard Business School Press; First edition 1999.

The Experience Economy, With a New Preface by the Authors: Competing for Customer Time, Attention, and Money by B. Joseph Pine II and James H. Gilmore. Harvard Business Review Press; New edition 2019.

Fabled Service: Ordinary Acts, Extraordinary Outcomes by Betsy Sanders. Pfeiffer & Co; 1997.

The Five Temptations of a CEO, Anniversary Edition: A Leadership Fable by Patrick Lencioni. Jossey-Bass; First Edition 2008.

Holy Bible: New Living Translation. Tyndale; 2006.

How to Win Friends and Influence People by Dale Carnegie. Simon & Schuster; 1936.

If Disney Ran Your Hospital: 9 ½ Things You Would Do Differently by Fred Lee. Second River Healthcare; 2004.

Market-driven Health Care: Who Wins, Who Loses In The Transformation Of America's Largest Service Industry by Regina Herzlinger. Basic Books; First edition 1997.

Mass Affluence: Seven New Rules of Marketing to Today's Consumer by Paul Nunes and Brian Johnson. Harvard Business Review Press; 2004.

The New Gold Standard: 5 Leadership Principles for Creating a Legendary Customer Experience Courtesy of the Ritz-Carlton Hotel Company by Joseph Michelli. McGraw-Hill Education; First edition 2008.

The New Psychology of Money by Adiran Furnham. Routledge; 2014.

The Paradox of Choice by Barry Schwartz. EccoPress; Revised edition 2016.

Peak: How Great Companies Get Their Mojo from Maslow by Chip Conley. Wiley; Second edition 2017.

Physician Success Secrets: How the Best Get Better by Greg N. Korneluk. First edition 2004.

Purple Cow: Transform Your Business by Being Remarkable by Seth Godin. Penguin Books; 1st edition 2007.

Secret Service: Hidden Systems That Deliver Unforgettable Customer Service by John DiJulius. AMACOM; 2003.

Selling the Invisible: A Field Guide to Modern Marketing by Harry Beckwith. Grand Central Publishing; Reprint edition 2012.

Setting The Table: The Transforming Power of Hospitality in Business by Danny Meyer. Ecco; Reprint edition 2008.

The Seven Habits of Highly Effective People: Powerful Lessons in Personal Change by Stephen Covey. DC Books; 1994.

Small Giants: Companies That Choose to Be Great Instead of Big by Bo Burlingham. Portfolio; First edition 2005.

So What?: How to Communicate What Really Matters to Your Audience by Mark Magnacca. FT Press; First edition 2009.

The Substance of Style: How the Rise of Aesthetic Value Is Remaking Commerce, Culture, and Consciousness by Virginia Postrel. Harper Perennial; First edition 2004.

Ten Types of Innovation: The Discipline of Building Breakthroughs by Larry Keelye, et al. Wiley; First edition 2013. (The Doblin Group 5E Model on Compelling Experiences)

The Tipping Point: How Little Things Can Make a Big Difference by Malcolm Gladwell. Back Bay Books; 2002.

The 22 Immutable Laws of Marketing: Violate Them at Your Own Risk! by Al Ries and Jack Trout. HarperBusiness; First edition 1994.

What's the Secret?: To Providing a World-Class Customer Experience by John Di Julius. Wiley; 2008.

Whole-Scale Change: Unleashing the Magic in Organizations by Dannemiller Tyson Associates. Berrett-Koehler; 2000.

Why We Buy: The Science of Shopping by Paco Underhill. Simon & Schuster; Updated, Revised edition 2008.

Word of Mouth Marketing: How Smart Companies Get People Talking by Andy Sernovitz. Pressbox; Fourth edition 2015.

Zingerman's Guide to Giving Great Service by Ari Weinzweig. Hyperion; First edition 2004.

Articles

"Are You Undervaluing Customer Service?" 1st Financial Training Service.
https://www.1stfinancialtraining.com/Newsletters/trainerstoolkit1Q2009.pdf

"Closing the Delivery Gap" by James Allen, et al. Bain & Company. 2005.
https://www.bain.com/contentassets/41326e0918834cd1a0102fdd0810535d/bb_closing_delivery_gap.pdf

"The Elective Medical Procedure Payment Problem" by PYMNTS. 2019.
https://www.pymnts.com/healthcare/2019/solving-the-50b-elective-medical-procedure-payments-problem/

"The escape-room games industry is booming" by C.R. and A.W. 2019.
https://www.economist.com/gulliver/2019/01/11/the-escape-room-games-industry-is-booming

Golden Rule Chronology:
https://www.harryhiker.com/chronology.htm

"Healthcare Consumer Insight & Digital Engagement Survey Results Unveiled". 2018. https://www.binaryfountain.com/news/second-annual-healthcare-consumer-insight-digital-engagement-survey-results-unveiled/

"How Patients Use Online Reviews" by Lisa Hedges. 2019 https://www.softwareadvice.com/resources/how-patients-use-online-reviews/

"Questions of the Experience Economy: What You Ask Your Customers Defines What Business You Are In" by Kevin Dulle. 2019. https://www.linkedin.com/posts/kevindulle_visualtranslation-experienceeconomy-business-activity-6587695023003889664-BAaa

"What Are You Really Saying? The Importance of Nonverbal Clues" by Scott Anders. 2018. https://www.physicianleaders.org/news/what-are-you-really-saying-importance-nonverbal-clues

"Wine Study Shows Price Influences Perception" Caltech. 2008. https://www.caltech.edu/about/news/wine-study-shows-price-influences-perception-1374

Acknowledgements

Writing a book is a labor of love. As I've learned, it takes focus and discipline as well as a willingness to start, stop and start again. That's kind of how life works, isn't it? For many years, I resisted putting my passion for helping doctors into a single piece of work. I'm fortunate to have a number of people who have guided me along the way, their help ranging from gentle prodding to an outright proverbial kick in the backside.

First are the doctors who have been reading my monthly columns, newsletters and posts. Over the years, many doctors and staff have offered kind words about the writing I've done and the impact it's made on their practices. Jon and Sandy were the first to tell me directly to write a book and their words stuck with me.

I've been fortunate to meet a bunch of authors over the years, each of whom shared their own experiences in getting their work written, edited and published. John D., Jim, Chip, Debra,

Peter, Dean, and John B. all come to mind. The common take-away from each of these authors is to make the work mine.

When I returned to full time consulting several years ago, I was the beneficiary of some great coaching by my colleague Kathy, whose words of advice were reminiscent of the iconic Nike slogan, "Just Do It." Her help in framing the content as a series of insights made it possible for me to write and then write some more each day.

Several doctors agreed to read the manuscript, which is a consuming task. I appreciate Vance and Steve for the time they gave. The content is definitely better because of their comments and feedback.

And with the help of Nathan, my publishing team materialized: Jeremy, Amy, David and Alyssa worked hard to get this book over the finish line and bring it to life!

I also got some nice help along the way with formatting and editing from Kennedy and Avery, my two daughters, along with daily care and feeding offered by my wife Renée, who is the Chief Encouragement Officer of our family.

I thank you.

How are you going BEYOND?

We want to hear from you!

The main goal of this book is to inspire doctors and their teams to take the patient experience to a new level in their practices.

Share your stories with the author for possible inclusion as a case study planned for the next edition of *Beyond Bedside Manner*.

Email: stories@sm2strategic.com
Phone: SM2 Strategic (925) 425-9900

Learn what others are doing.

- See interviews, videos, and podcasts with doctors and team members at practices that have a strong patient experience culture.
- Explore new ideas resulting from putting these insights into practice.
- Build a strong patient experience culture within your practice with interactive training for the entire team.

Visit *www.beyondbedsidemanner.com*

About the Author

Shareef Mahdavi is founder and president of SM2 Strategic, a firm dedicated to optimizing the patient experience. Early in his career Shareef led the marketing launch of the laser platform used in LASIK eye surgery, the most widely performed elective surgical procedure worldwide.

As a consultant, researcher and speaker, he has helped hundreds of medical practices and also advises medical companies ranging from start-ups to Fortune 500s. He has authored more than 100 articles and reports on the growth of elective services and is a recognized expert on The Experience Economy.

He and his wife Reneé reside in Pleasanton, California, where they raised their three children and enjoy living and working as part of the vibrant downtown community.

To contact the author directly; shareef@sm2strategic.com

Made in the USA
Las Vegas, NV
16 May 2022

48964843R00149